CONTENTS

A young John Wayne seated on a white horse in an apparently mid-west locale in this publicity handout

"Wayne was an artist of considerable versatility"

INTRODUCTION

THE LEGEND OF John Wayne is alive and well to this day, even 30 years after his death. He is an actor whose contribution to cinema cast a monumental shadow, a performer whose identity is preserved on screen and in public. His name and image are everywhere. Travellers are welcomed by an impressive bronze statue of the star on arrival at John Wayne Airport in Orange County, California, whose Sheriff's Department also pays tribute to the icon with its Duke helicopters. Wayne was a giant of a man – both literally and figuratively – and an artist of considerable versatility who enjoyed immense popularity overseas and also at home in America. Motion Picture Exhibitors garlanded Wayne with the Laurel Award for Topline Star in 1949 – the

year that also coincided with his first Oscar nomination – and Wayne's outstanding contribution to the world of entertainment was celebrated in 1966 with the Hollywood Foreign Press Association's Cecil B DeMille award. Deserved recognition indeed for a formidable screen presence who made well in excess of 175 feature films in a distinguished career that lasted for almost 50 years as a star, and saw Wayne work in the business during six different decades. His record speaks for itself. In the compulsive 1980 guide, *The Guinness Book of Film Facts and Feats*, author Patrick Robertson bestows on Wayne the coveted gold medal as "The Hollywood star who played the most leading roles in feature films" – 142, apparently, between 1927 and

1976. Such a consistent appearance in the limelight would reveal Wayne to be one of the most significant box-office attractions Hollywood has ever known. In addition, votes down the years from the American public brought endorsement to the statistics. Wayne's durability was confirmed by adoration. In 1950, 1951 and 1954, he was the proud winner of the annual Quigley Poll, in which cinema exhibitors determined their top 10 box-office draws for that year. Wayne was an accomplished second in the 1963 Poll as well, the decade that judged him the overall winner. When it boils down to seats sold, you can't dispute the figures. Appeal never lies, and the public is always the harshest critic or the most devoted supporter.

John Wayne talking with Captain Peter Dawkins in Saigon during the filming of The Green Berets

Away from the cameras, however, Wayne was unpopular in some areas for his political views, and much has been made of this. He was President of the Motion Picture Alliance for the Preservation of American Ideals, the organisation founded in 1943, one of whose major concerns at the time was that "this industry is made up of, and dominated by, communists, radicals and crackpots". Wayne was staunchly right wing, and his sympathies were Republican. He was a supporter of President Richard Nixon and also an outspoken opponent of communism. In the final analysis, though, a performer should be judged on his performances, and I shall mainly be exploring Wayne the actor. Let the politicians be scrutinised for their politics. I would also add that "crackpots" are far more relevant to the Hollywood equation, and far more dominant. The madness of the Californian movie-making factory will never dissipate. Nor will the magnitude of John Wayne, a colossal, enduring star who ascended the ladder of Hollywood's finest after his inauspicious start as a prop assistant. Wayne became an idol for millions and his influence extended way beyond the various characters he portrayed on screen. Fortitude and individualism will forever be associated with Wayne, and those virtues that helped to construct a nation became Wayne's trademark throughout his glittering career. With time, fiction and truth coalesced as essential elements in the Wayne myth. Life had imitated art to such an extent that legend and man appeared inseparable. This is the man, remember, who was described in his screen infancy by director John Ford as "this new kid with a funny walk, like he owned the world." Near enough.

Outside view of the house where John Wayne was born on 26 May, 1907

Marion Robert Morrison alias John Wayne, as a baby

EARLY YEARS

ON 26TH MAY 1907, the man who would achieve global recognition as John Wayne, and become one of cinema's most illustrious stars, was born Marion Robert Morrison in the small town of Winterset, Iowa. The second name of Robert was soon adjusted to Michael in favour of Marion's younger brother, who became known himself as Robert. Nevertheless, this middle alteration seems to have had no effect on Marion, who suggested in later years that his Christian name, rather – the unmanly Marion – was a far heavier cross to bear for a young boy growing up. Now, however, Marion is an integral part of the early Wayne identity. The childhood home at 216 South Second Street stands as a powerful memorial to the man and his achievements, and is open seven days a week to the public. Hundreds of thousands of devotees have made pilgrimage to this shrine. Painted white, the modest house sits quietly, the billowing American flag keeping faithful vigil outside. The décor within conforms to the style of the period, and there are letters from assorted stars, photographs and film memorabilia relating to one of America's most famous sons. Tours of the property are available, too, and the shop houses a variety of Duke merchandise: there are even John Wayne luggage tags on sale. This is where Wayne began his journey to greatness, but the Winterset days were short-lived.

"He realised rapidly
that performing
was his calling"

"Marion acquired the nickname of 'Duke'"

Marion's Presbyterian father Clyde Leonard was a pharmacist by trade, and soon moved with wife Mary and the children to the sunnier climes of California for health reasons. There was an unsuccessful time ranching out in the desert, before Clyde finally settled the family in Glendale, Los Angeles, when Marion was still a child. Here, early jobs for the lad included selling newspapers and working as a delivery boy for his father, and it was at this formative stage of his life that Marion seems to have acquired the nickname of "Duke", which followed him into later years as a mark of distinction. The provenance of the title is slightly confused: Wayne the star would laugh off any implications of blue blood in the moniker, and some evidence suggests that he played a duke on the boards at Glendale High School. Nevertheless, the general consensus would have it that Marion was called Duke after his favourite childhood terrier. The Glendale firemen are said to have noticed the inseparable pair, and thus Marion was first 'baptised' as "Little Duke", and thereafter with just the name of his pet dog.

Marion was soon a strapping teenager – photographs reveal an athletic young man carved out of granite – and he won a sporting scholarship to the University of Southern California in 1925, following rejection from his first-choice destination, the US Naval Academy. A competent football-player and member of the 1924 Glendale High champion team, Marion was spotted during his college years by silent western star Tom Mix. The kindly actor then gave the rookie a helping hand in the direction of the movie business with a summer job shifting props at Fox – allegedly in exchange for coveted match tickets. Born in Pennsylvania in 1880, Mix was a former Wild West show performer who already enjoyed an established place within the film industry. A masterful horseman, Mix had started out in pictures as a stockman, extra and stunt-crew member with the Selig Company in 1909, before crossing over to develop a stellar career with Fox in 1917. He was a debonair, dashing hero of this era – aided and abetted by his trusty equine companion, Tony – and is crowned in many quarters as the cowboy king of the silent western. He enjoyed enormous popular appeal and as a famous superstar on the Fox payroll in 1925, he was commanding a princely sum in the region of 17,000 dollars per week. In 1940, Mix died in a car crash in Florence, Arizona. The scene of the accident commemorates the star with a statue of a riderless horse. Mix is gone, but by no means forgotten.

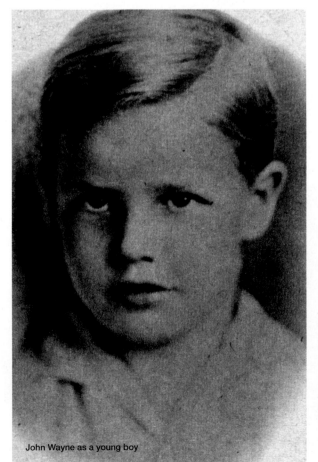

John Wayne as a young boy

Pioneering Western actor Tom Mix in action in 1920. Mix was an inspiration to John Wayne in the early days

"An athletic man carved out of granite"

Given his intro by Mix, Marion slowly began to learn about the craft of film-making behind the scenes. 1927 saw him make an uncredited appearance on the football picture *The Drop Kick*, and there was further work that year for director John Ford in *Mother Machree*, where Marion enjoyed the dual role of prop assistant and geese-herding extra. Such unglamorous beginnings then led to further off-camera duties on *Four Sons* (1928) as well as an extra part in the black-and-white silent melodrama from Fox, *Hangman's House*. John Ford directed, Marion displayed his enthusiasm on screen as an excited race spectator, and future collaborator Victor McLaglen was billed miles ahead of him in the pecking order. Yet by 1929, Marion's apprenticeship seemed to be paying off. *In Words and Music*, he enjoyed a tiny role and the satisfaction of his first screen credit – on this occasion as Duke Morrison – and there was an opportunity for the actor to demonstrate his physical ability, too, with a small part in the John Ford football film, *Salute*. Sport was an activity that satisfied Duke's strong male instincts, and he realised rapidly that performing was his calling, as it allowed him to display his masculinity on camera. While working on *Salute*, Duke found himself in the genial company of future Ford regular, Ward Bond: the stocky American would add ballast and engaging touches of humour to various 'John Wayne' features in the future, and would become a star in his own right with the popular 1950s television series, *Wagon Train*.

John Wayne holding a rifle in a publicity photo for the movie Shepherd of the Hills, 1941

BIG BREAK INTO THE WILDERNESS

DUKE'S BREAKTHROUGH and bid for stardom arrived finally in 1930, following a recommendation by John Ford to larger-than-life, one-eyed director Raoul Walsh. In the critical context of cinema, Walsh is esteemed by the French, and lauded for his direction of Jimmy Cagney's mother-fixated gangster in *White Heat* (1949), as well as eliciting magnificent performances from the wonderful Errol Flynn: *They Died with Their Boots On* (1941), *Gentleman Jim* (1942) and *Objective, Burma!* (1945). Born in New York in 1887, Walsh was the most colourful of characters. In his formative years, the half-Spanish, half-Irish American had been both a cowboy and a sailor,

and had participated as an actor for the legendary director DW Griffith in his *Birth of a Nation* (1915).

A wrangler of considerable expertise, Walsh has been credited in some circles with co-directing the first western talkie, the Fox-Movietone production *In Old Arizona* (1928). Also, it was Walsh who introduced the blossoming actor Duke Morrison to the rudimentary skills of horsemanship and gunplay. He had spotted the burly prop assistant transporting a huge chair above his head with great panache, and John Ford had intimated too that Morrison possessed special qualities.

John Wayne on the set of The Big Stampede, 1932

"The legend that would crystallise as John Wayne was born"

John Wayne in his first leading role as Breck Coleman in The Big Trail, 1930

Walsh then cast Morrison as the lead male of his film *The Big Trail*, for which he first suggested that the young unknown change his screen identity to Anthony Wayne, before the legend that would crystallise as John Wayne was born. As director, Walsh would collaborate again with Wayne on the wartime picture *Dark Command* (1940), and he would go on to become one of the most prolific and admired old-timers in the business. Walsh's 1964 cavalry western *A Distant Trumpet* would mark the end of a distinguished career behind the camera, but back in 1930, *The Big Trail* was no success, critically or commercially. Although the movie benefited from memorable outdoor scenes of a wagon train on the Oregon trail – Wayne starred as scout Breck Coleman with co-star Marguerite Churchill and Ward Bond along for the journey – the epic production was scuppered to some degree by its scale.

Presented in the panoramic 70mm Grandeur process – a format that many cinema theatres of the day could not accommodate, this costly early talkie flopped, and was described as "often stagey" by *Theatre Magazine*. Wayne now resigned himself with stoicism to a further nine long years developing his technique in the good-versus-evil land of the B-western. Although laborious at times, this was a period of paramount importance that cultivated the Duke's characteristic screen persona of a rugged, no-nonsense individual – a

tough, courageous man who stood up proudly for the values of justice and fair play.

The 1930s would prove a most prolific time in Wayne's working life. He churned out scores of negligible films under the banner of studios such as Republic, Mascot and Columbia, and also entered the domain of the serial. *The Hurricane Express* and *Shadow of the Eagle* appeared in 1932, and the year after brought *The Three Masketeers*, as well as a different Wayne debut in *Riders of Destiny* – the first of the Singin' Sandy westerns for Monogram, dubbed voice and all! This was a character that Wayne would most certainly rather forget, and one that stood in poor company alongside his macho roles of later years. There was no evidence yet of a star on show during this decade of toil, and feature titles such as *The Trail Beyond* (1934), *The Lonely Trail* (1936) and *Pals of the Saddle* (1938) indicate the locale of Wayne's product.

It would appear that John Wayne was trotting slowly into obscurity on a one-plot horse until director John Ford picked him up again for *Stagecoach*, the 1939 western that would reposition the genre as an admirable entertainment. More importantly, Wayne's collaboration at this particular moment with the crusty, opinionated Ford would aid in the gradual perfection of his distinctive image, and launch him on a journey towards stardom and screen immortality.

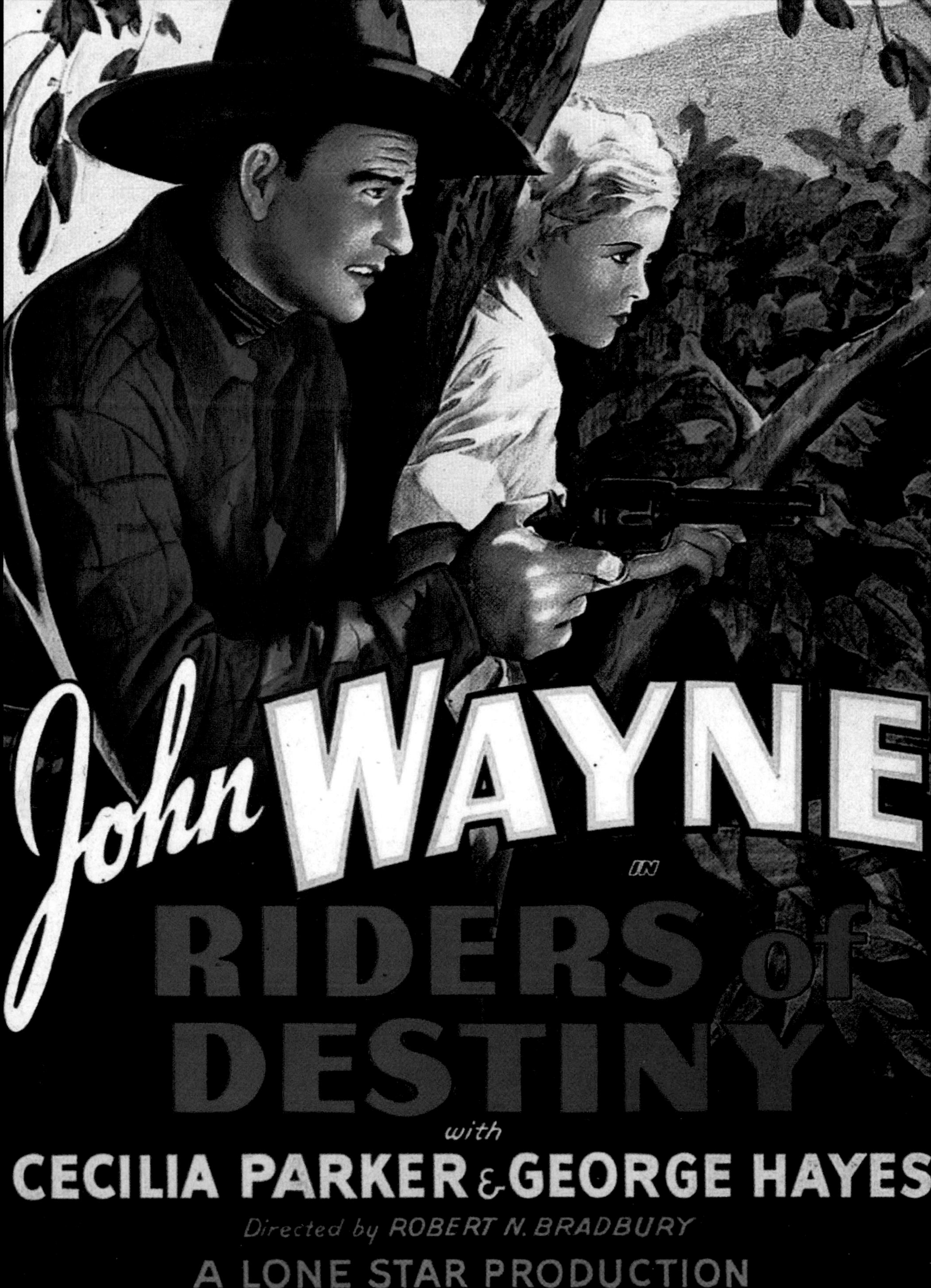

JOHN **WAYNE**

IN

RIDERS of DESTINY

with
CECILIA PARKER & **GEORGE HAYES**
Directed by ROBERT N. BRADBURY
A LONE STAR PRODUCTION

John Wayne (Ringo Kid) and Claire Trevor (Dallas) in Stagecoach, 1939

Film director and cinema legend
John Ford in 1942

A STAR IS BORN

"Stagecoach was the film that gave the western respectability"

JOHN FORD WAS an American-born Irishman of immigrant parents. He was already an Oscar success by 1939, his IRA drama *The Informer* having won him the best director award of 1935. A painter of evocative moving pictures with respected experience in westerns, Ford had not ventured into the genre for 13 years – his land-rush spectacular *Three Bad Men* was by now a distant memory of 1926. *Stagecoach*, therefore, established a series of firsts for both director John Ford and his chosen principal, John Wayne. This would be Wayne's initial starring performance under Ford, even though the duo had collaborated previously for 1927's *Mother Machree* and *Hangman's House* in 1928. Ford definitely wanted Wayne for the *Stagecoach* part of the Ringo Kid – a determined outlaw on a mission to avenge his murdered brother – and the masterful creation that emerged from their combined talents was the solidification of a friendly partnership that would result in various cinematic gems.

John Wayne as the Ringo Kid in John Ford's
first sound western, Stagecoach

George Bancroft, John Wayne and Louise Platt making their way through dangerous Apache territory in Wayne's breakthrough movie, Stagecoach, 1939

The western would be prominent in their pairing, and Stagecoach saw Ford's view of the Old West complemented for the first time by the stunning backdrop of Monument Valley, Utah, a dust-choked, desolate landscape of breathtaking beauty. The location would be associated indelibly with Ford.

As a film, *Stagecoach* is an experience to be enjoyed on many levels. King of the movie critics, Barry Norman, includes it among his 100 best works of the last century – alongside two other John Wayne westerns, *Red River* (Howard Hawks, 1948) and *The Searchers* (John Ford again, 1956). Norman explains: "Westerns even more than musicals are America's outstanding contribution to the cinema; the best of them are not just exciting adventure stories but modern morality plays." Morality is at the heart of *Stagecoach*, and Norman mentions notably how it was "the film that gave the western respectability."

There are other avenues to explore. Although a sturdy, uncompromising individual, Wayne's character Ringo is that rare combination of bravery and tenderness. Having joined the travelling party mid-passage – Ford's camera thrusts Wayne upon audiences by zooming in as he brandishes his Winchester rifle – Ringo shows remarkable kindness and good manners to the prostitute, Dallas (Claire Trevor). She has been drummed out of town and obliged to accompany the motley assortment of stagecoach passengers on their journey through hostile Apache terrain. Ringo attends to Dallas respectfully – offering her a seat at table and water en route – and only

Thomas Mitchell's alcohol-sodden doctor joins Ringo in treating Dallas with dignity. However, the jolly medic Josiah Boone's mind is set firmly on the bottle, and little else. Mitchell took home the 1939 best supporting actor Oscar for his performance, but the film was ousted from the year's best picture position by *Gone with the Wind*.

Ford's genius would be recognised by the Academy on three more occasions. His best director nods for *The Grapes of Wrath* (1940), *How Green Was My Valley* (1941), a rosy portrait of a Welsh mining community, and *The Quiet Man* (1952) – one of Wayne's most popular star vehicles – place Ford on his own pedestal in movie history. To this day, his unique record remains intact, and his achievement stands alone. Ford is the only man to have received the Oscar for best director four times. He had a marvellous eye, and his stories are regularly enhanced by impressive landscapes – the timeless mystique of Monument Valley, the emerald splendour of Ireland – as well as an eccentric squadron of supporting players. When the action comes too thick and fast in the Ford universe, these characters are likely to materialise and balance the equation with humour. Ford's detractors criticise the man for sentimentality and playing too liberally with Western history, but I am more than content in Ford's case to see the legend printed instead of fact. If cinema is to be viewed as an entertainment medium, then John Ford should be considered one of its greatest entertainers. Following his death in 1973, he was honoured with the Life Achievement in Motion Pictures Award by the American Film Institute.

Twenty-five years into the future, the 1998 poll of the Top 100 American Films conducted by the same organisation saw *Stagecoach* rattle in proudly at number 63 – sandwiched by *Tootsie* above and *Close Encounters* below. Surprisingly, however, Wayne and Ford's later masterpiece The Searchers (1956) was left straggling far behind in critical no-man's-land at number 96.

With *Stagecoach*, John Ford had finally deposited Wayne at stardom's door, and two other team-members are more than deserving of mention. Producer Walter Wanger went on later in his career to oversee *Cleopatra* (1963), the $40-million spectacular with Elizabeth Taylor and Richard Burton. Stuntman extraordinaire Yakima Canutt reserved his place in collective memory as well with the thrilling stagecoach chase sequence across the salt flats of the Mojave desert. Firstly, the fearless daredevil and rider – heavily disguised as one of Geronimo's braves – leaps from his galloping steed onto the team of horses, before passing back underneath the thundering transport. Secondly, Canutt stands in for the Ringo Kid, who jumps from the carriage before proceeding down the harness line to settle the bolting black chargers. In the current stunt climate of secure wirework and blue-screen aerodynamics, they don't make men in the Canutt mould any more. The master wrangler committed even greater wonders to the screen over the years. Along with Andrew Marton, Canutt was second-unit supremo for the death-defying chariot race in *Ben-Hur* (1959), director William Wyler's multi-Oscar-winning extravaganza for MGM. Canutt was on scintillating form again in 1961's *El Cid*. As second-unit director for Anthony Mann, he orchestrated the climactic battle scenes on the beaches near to Valencia. Was Charlton Heston ever served so well?

John Wayne, Jeffrey Hunter and
Natalie Wood in The Searchers, 1956

Walter Pidgeon, Claire Trevor and John Wayne in Dark Command, 1940

"An endearing hero of raw education and simple values"

GEMINI RISING

HAVING ATTAINED THE stellar position that had escaped him for the better part of a decade, Wayne was reunited with *Stagecoach* co-star Claire Trevor and *The Big Trail* director Raoul Walsh in 1940. The Republic historical western *Dark Command* had been constructed specifically as a vehicle for Wayne, with its action unfolding in Kansas before the American Civil War. Slowly gaining in confidence by now, Wayne starred as Bob Seton, an endearing hero of raw education and simple values who sold himself to the town's electorate with those admirable Wayne qualities of earthy charm and good-natured humour:

"True I don't know much about the law. Ain't had much book learning. But the good Lord gave me a nose for smelling a horse thief a mile off. And what you need in these parts is a marshal that's better at smelling than spelling." The upstanding Seton goes on to

conclude: "But remember this. Before you can triumph o'er anything, you gotta catch it. I can catch it." Approved by the public, the newly elected federal marshal adheres to his first promises by confronting wicked Walter Pidgeon and his posse of outlaws, even if a late-night shoot-out with that opponent is required. Such was the stoical nature of the Wayne persona, and *Dark Command* would strengthen this. Additionally, further collaborations would ensue with Trevor. In 1954, the pair would team up together for William Wellman on *The High and the Mighty*. The respected director had by then seen his 1927 feature *Wings* win the first Oscar for best film, and in 1931 he had seared Jimmy Cagney into audience consciousness with his gangster drama *The Public Enemy* – still remembered for Cagney's brutality at breakfast, where he squashes a grapefruit into Mae Clarke's face.

The High and the Mighty was a huge success. Although Wayne's skyward roles would mainly be associated with the military in the 1940s and 1950s, Wellman's star-studded disaster movie provided the tailor-made location to demonstrate the Duke's dependability in a crisis. Released by Warner Bros, the Wayne-Fellows production announced its pedigree with bold trailer titles: "From high on the all-time best seller list, a mighty adventure soars to screen acclaim! High adventure that spans 3000 miles of danger." The trailer itself teased with the promise of excitement: "One by one they boarded the plane. The most bizarre group of people ever thrown together by fate on the most exciting adventure that ever spanned an ocean. There was Dan, who had used up his nine lives and was starting on number ten. May, who could talk to a man without saying a word..." The stage was now set, and in a part originally intended for Spencer Tracy, Wayne's Dan Roman – a co-pilot burdened with tragedy – was the epitome of cool. Co-star and principal pilot Robert Stack would lampoon his tough-talking image in the 1980 disaster spoof *Airplane!*, while Trevor (as May) and female cast member Jan Sterling each received 1954 Oscar nominations for best supporting actress. Although the duo were both serious 'contenders', they were beaten to the prize by Eva Marie Saint for her display opposite the mercurial Marlon Brando in director Elia Kazan's *On the Waterfront*. Wayne was absent from the Academy's list of nominees that year, but his gutsy portrayal of the heroic Roman – a complex individual rising to the challenge on the stricken San Francisco-bound passenger plane – confirmed his exalted status as the darling of America's cinema-going public.

"The most bizarre group of people ever thrown together by fate"

Claire Trevor and John Wayne in action in Raoul Walsh's Dark Command, 1940

John Wayne and Robert Stack in The High and the Mighty, 1954

In the same year as *Dark Command*, Wayne returned to the familiar company of director John Ford, stepping away now from the stage of the Kansas setting and off onto the mighty ocean in *The Long Voyage Home* (1940). Although the production placed him on friendly ground – *Stagecoach* producer Walter Wanger was the guiding force, while Thomas Mitchell, Ward Bond and John Qualen (a future cast member of *The Searchers*) were game for the adventure – this outing was very much an untypical departure for Wayne. His casting as Swedish merchant seaman Ole Olsen proved a part that least represented his customary rough-hewn image, and there were passages where his character displayed fear and panic, emotions not usually found in the Wayne handbook.

Nevertheless, sailor Ole Olsen was meant to symbolise a homesick man not totally in control of his destiny, and Wayne made a decent attempt at his necessarily thick Swedish accent, as well, a rare occasion on which the Duke exchanged his sonorous American twang for a mellower European register. He emerged with reputation fully intact, and this claustrophobic account of seafaring peril –

based on four one-act plays by Eugene O'Neill – has acquired a loyal fan base. The atmospheric black-and-white shadows by cinematographer Gregg Toland (*Citizen Kane*) come highly recommended, and his contribution was nominated for an Oscar. As for Wayne, he would specialise from this moment on in gritty, masculine types who commanded events around them – heroes that were indispensable cogs of propaganda in the Hollywood war machine.

While the likes of James Stewart and Clark Gable soon jumped into uniform for the American cause – the former as a steely bomber pilot, the latter as the idol of Peterborough town centre on one memorable occasion! – Wayne did not enlist. Reasons for his absence are legion, most notably his married status and age at the time, as well as the non-priority draft postponement requested by Republic Studios for Wayne's support of national health, safety or interest. One source even suggests that the Duke was refused military service because of deafness in one ear. Surely it was more beneficial, though, to leave Wayne behind to play the most important roles of his life? We all need our supermen.

John Wayne starring in Flying Tigers, a 1942 war film about a mercenary fighter pilot battling the Japanese in China

"Fear and panic, emotions not usually found in the Wayne handbook"

WAYNE
ROLL ★ ANNA LEE

"NG TIGERS"

PAUL KELLY
GORDON JONES
MAE CLARKE
BILL SHIRLEY

DAVID MILLER Director
Screen play by
Kenneth Gamet · Barry Trivers
Original story by Kenneth Gamet
Associate Producer
EDMUND GR

A
REPUBLIC

Scene from Long Voyage Home in 1940 with
Ward Bond, John Ford, Thomas Mitchell,
Jack Pennick, John Gualen and John Wayne

With the world exploding in conflict and the United States a recent addition to the fray, Wayne was the definitive star choice for films that required an all-American boy to embrace combat in the pursuit of freedom. If there was ever one man suitable to fight for good against evil, it was Wayne, and he launched himself into a variety of parts that epitomised the courage of a fierce, patriotic citizen. Battle would plot an uncharted course for Wayne, a perilous direction that would help to solidify the legend. He became America's most flamboyant protector when he took Hollywood to the front, and the hard-driving, tough-talking, flag-waving seriousness had a particular purpose: the job was winning. What he said on the screen, he believed off it,

and the Big John message was clear: "If you follow me and live by my standards, we can win this together."

Such an inspired declaration of intent became the nation's credo during those troubled years, and the performances matched the rhetoric. In director David Miller's *Flying Tigers* (1942), a hearty morale-booster from Republic Studios, Wayne took to the skies as grizzled squadron leader Jim Gordon, in an action-packed story about American servicemen engaging the Japanese on behalf of China. As the cynical military commander, Wayne encapsulated the individual who was ready to sacrifice his own popularity for the sake of ultimate victory.

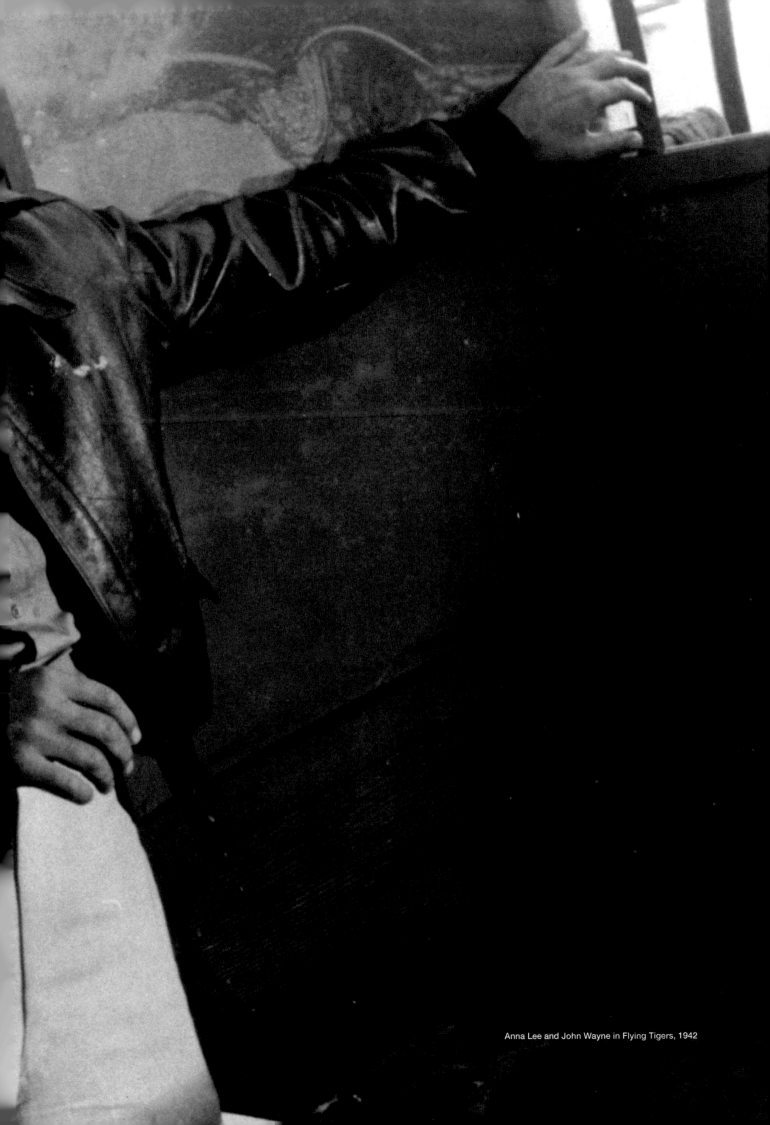

Anna Lee and John Wayne in Flying Tigers, 1942

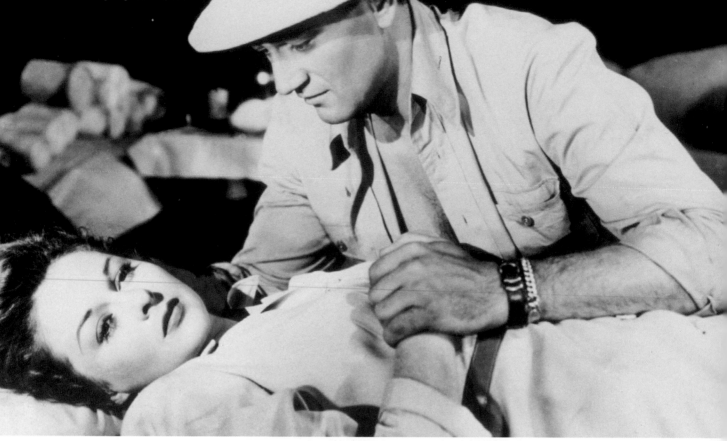

Susan Hayward and John Wayne in a scene from Fighting Seabees, 1944

The heroics continued, as Wayne exemplified the ordinary warrior standing up defiantly as a courageous tool against the forces of oppression. In director Edward Ludwig's *The Fighting Seabees* (1944), he proved himself as a man so committed to winning that he would undertake any risk at any price – so much so that he would be prepared to die willingly for the flag. Here Wayne was in combative mode again with the Japanese, making a major contribution to the Republic war effort with his part as win-at-all-costs construction worker Wedge Donovan, an individual experiencing hell in the Pacific. This was a guy from the top drawer that you undoubtedly wanted on your side. "They'll be back. Hold your fire till you get 'em under your guns. Then let 'em have it!" After issuing these instructions to a colleague during the beachfront battle, he takes a digger to incinerate a fuel dump at the centre of the conflict, perishing valiantly in a hail of machine-gun fire before the site erupts in a ball of flame.

"The ordinary warrior standing up defiantly against the forces of oppression"

John Wayne and Dennis O'Keefe in Fighting Seabees, 1944

"Ford and Wayne were now poised for perfection"

John Wayne as Colonel Joseph Madden in Back to Bataan, 1945

Japan featured on Wayne's agenda once more in director Edward Dmytryk's rousing RKO flag-waver *Back to Bataan* (1945). This was Wayne's one-and-only picture with Dmytryk – a member of the "Hollywood Ten" who would refuse to reveal their alleged communist persuasions under questioning during the industry witch hunts in 1947, and an artist whose left-wing sympathies were in diametric opposition to the Duke's. Wayne starred as a responsible individual at the heart of the war who embodied the whole-hearted American virtues of compassion, decency and fortitude. Anthony Quinn offered solid support to Wayne's virile, no holds-barred hero Colonel Madden, a soldier leading forces of liberation against the Japanese in the occupied Philippines.

Ironically, it was then a Wayne movie dealing with the 1941 American retreat from the Philippines under General MacArthur

that had a rapturous welcome back home in 1945. Released in December of that year when the horrors of war were over, director and co-producer John Ford's *They Were Expendable* presented Wayne as characteristically resilient and uncompromising in the face of adversity. As Lieutenant RG "Rusty" Ryan, Wayne played second fiddle this time to principal star Robert Montgomery, and the MGM picture was Ford's heartfelt tribute to the fighting personnel of torpedo boats in the Pacific. Ford had been an active documentary-maker during the conflict, and became a rear admiral in the US Navy Reserve after the Second World War. Although the film concentrated on a mournful episode in American military history, the production benefited from newsreel-style authenticity, and paid worthy respect to the fallen. Ford and Wayne were now poised for perfection.

WAYNE THE MAGNIFICENT

AFTER THE SECOND World War, Wayne consolidated his manly image in the monumental cattle-drive western of 1948, *Red River*, with Howard Hawks at the helm. Born in Goshen, Indiana, in 1896, Hawks was a multi-talented director capable of operating with élan in several genres. In time he would be championed by the French as one of the finest *auteurs*, and he became the darling of the *Cahiers du Cinéma* critics. Hawks had many strings to his bow, and is often credited as being the inventor of overlapping dialogue in films – a machine-gun interchange of words most suited to the zany setting of the screwball comedy or the murky double-cross of *film noir*. Hawks's majestic canon of work is a roll-call of superlatives: *Scarface* (1932, well before the arrival of a scenery-chomping Al Pacino); *Bringing Up Baby* (1938); *The Outlaw* (1940, with Jane Russell bursting onto the screen

and out of her shirt); *To Have and Have Not* (1944); and Russell again, in this instance as a good-time gal with a flawless Marilyn Monroe in *Gentlemen Prefer Blondes* (1953). When Hawks died in 1977 – the same year that witnessed the demise of Groucho Marx and Charlie Chaplin – the light had finally been turned out on another of cinema's most dazzling contributors. In *Red River*, Hawks's first significant western that portrays a bygone era without sentimentality, Wayne played the part of tough cattle drover Tom Dunson, a seasoned pro whose experience is to be challenged by his foster-son Matt – a wonderful performance from the young Montgomery Clift. This was a massive picture painted on a broad, epic canvas, immortalised by the panoramic sweeps over the early-morning cattle before the drive begins, and dealt with the clash of generations.

John Wayne, Montgomery Clift and Walter Brennan in Red River, 1948

John Wayne as Thomas Dunson in Howard Hawks' Red River, 1948

Wayne was the personification of steely maturity, while Clift – an actor whose luminous talent would be eclipsed by personal problems later in his troubled life – was a revelation, and more than a match for his hardened colleague. Memorable scenes from *Red River* include a magnificently staged Indian attack, Wayne proving quicker than John Ireland in a shoot-out, and the legendary coming-together of Wayne and Clift. With Hawks's *Rio Bravo* (1959), *Red River* emerged as a profound examination of both character and conflict, with the great West acting as backdrop. (The two films also profited from the creative partnership of cinematographer Russell Harlan and musical legend Dimitri Tiomkin). Three decades after Red River, author Keith Reader wrote in glowing terms about Wayne's performance, describing the Duke's display as "superbly tyrannical." Western maestro John Ford had definitely been impressed with the incident-laden picture on release, as well as its theme of family confrontation. Most revelatory to Ford, though, had been Wayne's authentic portrayal of character: "I never knew that big son of a bitch could act," remarked Ford famously to Hawks on seeing the film for the first time.

"Red River emerged as a profound examination of both character and conflict"

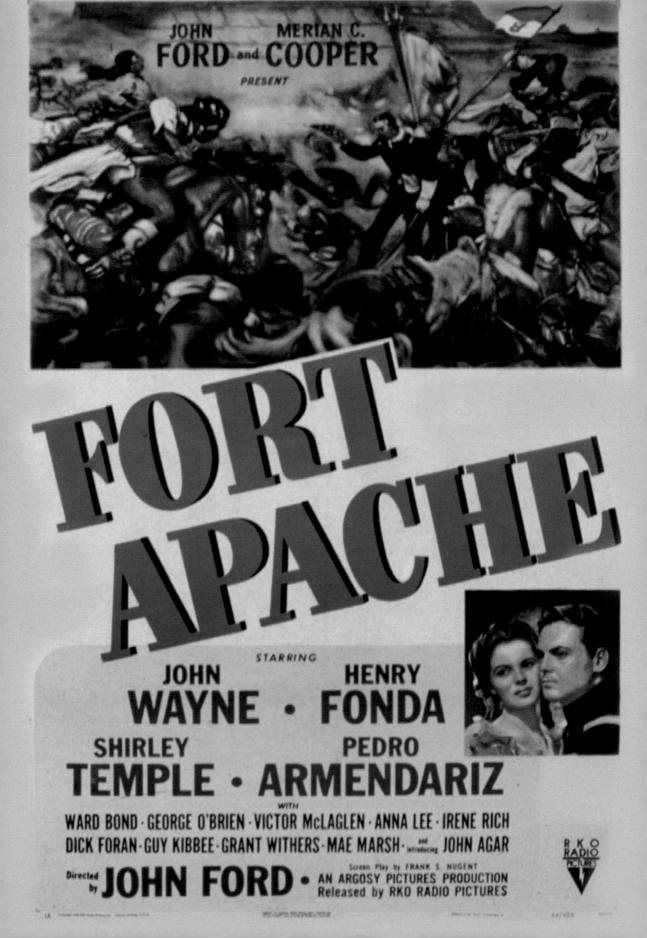

Henry Fonda in Fort Apache in 1948

A scene from Fort Apache, the first of John Ford's "cavalry trilogies" starring Henry Fonda, Shirley Temple, Ward Bond and John Wayne in 1948

"His complexity shone out in this darkly shaded role"

Wayne's acting prowess and considerable sincerity were demonstrated further in *Fort Apache* (1948), a pivotal moment in his career and the first instalment of director John Ford's esteemed cavalry trilogy. Wayne starred as Captain York, a military man characterised by his confident gait and belief in decency, and his complexity shone out in this darkly shaded role. Here was a dignified officer, a man of unquestionable principles who was destined to clash with his superior. Henry Fonda was the perfect incarnation of York's commanding officer, Lieutenant Colonel Owen Thursday. Bitter about his remote posting to the heart of the hostilities, Fonda's character was a bigoted, by-the-book disciplinarian whose narrow-minded hatred of the Indians would result in his

men falling victim to an Apache massacre. The conflict of ideals produced a memorable showdown. Wayne returned to camp in exultant spirits, but his attempts to broker peace with Apache chief Cochise were quashed by Fonda.

Wayne remained resolute, but he was confronted by a monolith of ignorance: "Colonel Thursday, I gave my word to Cochise. No man is going to make a liar out of me, sir." Fonda retaliates, blind to Wayne's qualities: "There's no question of honour, sir, between an American officer and Cochise." Wayne then lays down his credentials: "There is to me, sir," but the declaration falls on deaf ears, and later on Wayne is accused of cowardice by Fonda in their hypnotic Monument Valley confrontation. Wayne challenges Fonda to a

duel, who refuses: "I'm no duellist, Captain. I will decide whether I will answer you with pistols or a general court martial. You will remain on the ridge in safety, with the supply train." Although patronised to the point of insanity by Fonda, Wayne's character revealed subtle nuances. Having seen Thursday and his minions ride off to certain death, York was still prepared to maintain the US Cavalry's patriotic image of courage and duty. Thursday would be considered a hero for the sake of the regiment, and military reputation would be upheld. Wayne and his character exited from *Fort Apache* with heads held high in honour – while regular Ford participant and former boxer Victor McLaglen added stature and comic relief to the proceedings as the sentimental sergeant.

John Wayne in an intense fight scene from
Red River released in 1948

3 GODFATHERS

...AREY, JR.
...WARD BOND · MAE MARSH
...JANE DARWELL · BEN JOHNSON
DIRECTED BY JOHN FO...

COLOR BY TECHNICOLOR

SCREEN PLAY BY LAURENCE STALLINGS AND FRANK S. NUGENT · FROM THE STORY BY PETE...
PRODUCED BY ARGOSY PICTURES CORPORA...
A METRO-GOLDWYN-MAYER PICTURE

In contrast to the arduousness of *Red River* and the emotional jousting at the heart of *Fort Apache*, Wayne found himself in lighter mood that same year (1948) with John Ford's *Three Godfathers*. This sentimental escapade was a religious allegory of sorts, and dedicated to one of the director's most adored actors, Harry Carey Sr – "bright star of the early Western sky." A key figure of the silent western and a popular character actor in the Thirties, Bronx-born Carey had died the previous year after almost 40 years in the business, and his boyish-looking son, Harry Carey Jr, played one of an outlaw trio in *Three Godfathers* alongside the Duke and Pedro Armendáriz. The latter, a Mexican actor of some note, had supported Wayne in *Fort Apache*. Later in his career, he would appear with Sean Connery in *From Russia with Love*, and took his own life in 1963 instead of facing the pain of terminal illness. There was also a debut performance from future Ford-Wayne alumnus Ben Johnson. A former rodeo rider and film stockman, Johnson doubled occasionally for Wayne, and would appear as a star in his own right for

The Wild Bunch (1968). The story of *Three Godfathers*, which had already received various film outings since 1909, dealt with the problems encountered by the selfless Wayne, Armendáriz and Carey Jr as they took it upon themselves to care for an orphaned baby. The picture's outdoor beauty was rendered in loving Technicolor by ace cameraman Winton C Hoch, and, on solid form, Wayne ensured that his likeable character Robert Marmaduke Hightower cruised through this sugary concoction with the minimum of fuss.

1949 proved a similar year of cinematic contrasts for Wayne. In Republic's family-orientated picture *The Fighting Kentuckian* from director George Waggner – which Wayne also produced – he displayed his trademark good values with the appealing character of John Breen. This was a sturdy figure defending the rights of downtrodden settlers against land-grabbing crooks, and comedy royalty Oliver Hardy stood beside Wayne in a rare serious role.

Wayne was in sombre mood himself as John Ford's cavalry trilogy thundered on with its second episode, *She Wore a Yellow*

Ribbon (1949), a teary lament to the inevitability of age and the importance of friendship. With fortitude and resolve still guiding his distinctive screen image, Wayne inspired sympathy in his role of Captain Nathan Brittles, a gruff widower questioning the validity of his military mission. Here was a respected officer of some distinction, a man whose final undertaking was to deter local Indian insurgency, and for whom the reassuring camaraderie of stockade life was soon to be a distant shadow. It was a new experience for Wayne playing a person considerably older than his actual age, and he displayed moments of tenderness in golden-hued scenes where Brittles foresees the obstacles posed by his impending retirement and converses with his deceased wife at her grave. Wayne was particularly gentle as he watered the tombstone flowers lovingly, and revealed untapped levels of vulnerability: "Well Mary, only six more days to go and your old Nathan'll be out of the army." Here was the essential issue of the picture, a glowing meditation on comradeship, painted thickly on the sand-choked canvas of the Old West in 1876.

"Wayne inspired sympathy in his role of Captain Nathan Brittles"

Winton C Hoch's yellowy Technicolor cinematography complemented the nostalgic mood and received that year's Oscar. The *tour de force* sequence is undoubtedly the magnificent thunderstorm in Monument Valley – complete with heavenly forks of lightning – that Hoch photographed under pressure from John Ford. Hoch's magic would be called on again by the director for *The Quiet Man* (1952), where the cameraman would share Oscar honours with Archie Stout, and *The Searchers* (1956). Yet there are dramatic treasures on offer, too, in *She Wore a Yellow Ribbon*, Ford's quiet examination of a man on the verge of change: the palpable tension between fresh-faced cavalry officers Harry Carey Jr and John Agar – the one-time husband of Shirley Temple – and the humorous exchanges between Wayne and Ford regular, Victor McLaglen. An Oscar winner himself for Ford's *The Informer* (1935), the imposing McLaglen is best remembered as the man who would go a hundred rounds with Wayne in his hearty portrayal of Maureen O'Hara's brother in *The Quiet Man*. Passing mention should also be made to the lady of the yellow ribbon, Joanne Dru. In the previous year's Red River, she had been responsible for separating the fist-wielding Montgomery Clift and Wayne. Saving the best until last, however, the moment in *She Wore a Yellow Ribbon* where the veteran Brittles is presented with a commemorative watch from his troop – and reaches for his spectacles to read the inscription – is particularly moving. Wayne was developing his repertoire as an actor by now, and a landmark action role soon cemented his professional reputation.

"Wayne was tougher than nails in one of his most impressive performances"

John Wayne as Marine Sergeant John Stryker in the 1949 war film Sands of Iwo Jima

THE MARINES' GREATEST HOUR

A GREAT HUMAN STORY ...MAKES A MIGHTY MOTION PICTURE

SANDS OF IWO JIMA

JOHN WAYNE · JOHN AGAR · ADELE MARA · FORREST TUCKER

A REPUBLIC PICTURE

"Saddle up!" barked the Duke, and cinema audiences of 1949 prepared for a rough ride with one of Wayne's most iconic characters. This proved to be the year in which Wayne received his first Oscar nomination, and the Academy's recognition was well deserved. The success of *Stagecoach* was now 10 years in the past, and Wayne had matured. Directed by Allan Dwan, the Republic drama *Sands of Iwo Jima* was the ideal platform for Wayne's talents, and he rose to the challenge with distinction. The picture was an unapologetic – and extremely effective – memorial to American endeavour during the Pacific hell of World War II, and the Duke dominated the screen: "My name is Stryker. Sergeant John M Stryker. You're gonna be my squad!" Wayne was tougher than nails in one of his most impressive performances and Sergeant Stryker was no cardboard cut-out.

Charged with transforming novices into a deadly fighting unit, Wayne's fearless marine came across as a heroic leader of men whose resilience and courage were pinned proudly on his breast like medals. Nevertheless, the war-weary exterior concealed a protective nature. Stryker shouldered the immense responsibility of moulding his adoptive 'sons' into an effective combat machine, while simultaneously facing unbearable odds in battle. Here was an admirable symbol of American valour who would accept defeat at no cost – a campaign-hardened soldier ready to make the ultimate sacrifice for the cause. It wasn't really cricket to witness the Duke shot in the back, and

Wayne experienced further bad luck at the 1949 Academy Awards. Although many people had considered his charismatic turn as Stryker a dead cert for the best actor Oscar, Wayne lost out to Broderick Crawford in *The Hustler* director Robert Rossen's *All the King's Men*. You can't win 'em all, and Crawford's part was, ironically, a role that the Duke had himself refused. However, *Sands of Iwo Jima* had considerably enhanced Wayne's clout with the critics, and the movie-going public appreciated the no-holds-barred Stryker, who was in many respects an extension of the Duke in real life.

John Wayne on the charge in Sands of Iwo Jima, 1949

FROM MAUREEN TO ETHAN

WITH THE FLAG-waving success of *Iwo Jima* behind him, Wayne starred in *Rio Grande* in 1950, the concluding part of John Ford's cavalry trilogy. Here he delivered a sincere, moving performance as moustachioed Lieutenant Colonel Kirby Yorke, a resolute individual who placed his military obligations before family responsibility. Wayne brought his customary gravitas to the complex role of an experienced soldier protecting settlers from bellicose Indians during the Apache wars of the late-19th century. Yorke was also attempting to protect himself from his estranged wife, whose property he had razed to the ground during the American Civil War. Matters were complicated to an even greater degree earlier in the picture by the arrival of Yorke's son, Jeff (Claude Jarman Jr), who had flunked out of West Point and was desperate to sign up. One wondered just how long the married couple

could spat with one another, though, before adoration replaced anger, as the lady at the heart of this drama was Maureen O'Hara. Born in Dublin in 1920 as Maureen Fitzsimmons, the flame-haired Irish beauty with mesmerising green eyes had followed up her apprenticeship in the theatre with parts in British pictures – most notably for Alfred Hitchcock in 1939 with *Jamaica Inn*. O'Hara's subsequent transition to Hollywood had been swift, and her impact instantaneous. She had made a sympathetic heroine as the object of Charles Laughton's affections in William Dieterle's highly acclaimed *The Hunchback of Notre Dame* (1939). Also, she was a ravishing match for the swashbuckling Tyrone Power in Henry King's pirate entertainment *The Black Swan* (1942), and had worked with director John Ford prior to *Rio Grande* on his 1941 mining saga *How Green Was My Valley*.

"Wayne and O'Hara would be immortalised as a memorable screen couple"

O'Hara would join forces with Wayne and Ford for the 1952 Oscar winner *The Quiet Man*, and yet again for *The Wings of Eagles* in 1957. Her display in *The Long Gray Line* (1954) was remembered devotedly by author David Quinlan as "a four-handkerchief movie caressingly made by Ford and lifted to greatness by the performance of Maureen O'Hara." The actress's later partnerships with Wayne included her feisty role as the title character's shrewish wife in *McLintock!* (1963), and *Big Jake* (1971). With these latter collaborations and *Rio Grande*, Wayne and O'Hara would be immortalised as a memorable screen couple. They were firm friends off camera – Wayne was the personification of easy, relaxed charm when they met at a party – and their cinematic pairing revealed potent chemistry at work. As a duo, Wayne and the radiant O'Hara sit comfortably beside Fred and Ginger and Bogart and Bacall. Though invariably at loggerheads emotionally – and physically! – they are ultimately destined for reconciliation and mutual respect. The magic that they conjured up together on film endures, and is still electrifying today. Romantic tension between Wayne and O'Hara was constant in *Rio Grande*, but the conjugal fireworks were alleviated by exciting set pieces, particularly the Roman-riding contest between Harry Carey Jr and Ben Johnson. Victor McLaglen was in evidence, too, uncorking whimsy of characteristic vintage. Yet the entertainment was the Duke's show, and Yorke was a fully rounded character. Compassionate and understanding, Wayne was tough and tender in equal measure. As the officer facing up to responsibility, he was brave enough to take an arrow in the chest and have it pulled out. But he respected his own men and was not too proud to ask for their aid: "Son, help me to my horse."

John Wayne and Janet Leigh in the 1957 Cold War romantic Jet Pilot

John Wayne as Major Dan Kirby in Flying Leathernecks, 1951

Before setting off from America across the Atlantic with Maureen O'Hara and John Ford in tow for the colour-soaked spectacle of *The Quiet Man* in 1952, Wayne slipped out of his *Iwo Jima* battle dress and *Rio Grande* cavalry stripes and donned the uniform of the skies in two 1951 RKO films. *Flying Leathernecks* and *Jet Pilot* both saw the Duke airborne, always a reliable bet as the standard-bearer of courage. In the former, a standard Second World War action drama from director Nicholas Ray, Wayne was on loud-mouthed form as Major Dan Kirby, with co-star Robert Ryan adding contrast to the congratulatory heroics. The latter was a romantic drama from director Josef von Sternberg, and the aerial material on offer found Wayne's sky supremo Colonel Shannon besotted with Janet Leigh's Soviet fly girl. You couldn't make it up! The love-laden extravaganza that was *Jet Pilot* did not actually get a release until 1957, and deserves notice as a curio in the careers of its participants.

Janet Leigh and John Wayne in the 1957 Cold War romantic Jet Pilot

"Wayne preserves his roughhouse charm and emerges victoriously to win his darling."

A scene from The Quiet Man filmed at the west Ireland village of Cong. The production won director John Ford an Oscar

Later on, Wayne realises that his beloved O'Hara has no dowry: "There'll be no locks or bolts between us, Mary Kate, except those in your mercenary little heart," snarls the Duke, displaying tremendous reserves of passion as he pulls O'Hara towards him. The stage is set for the most memorable showdown, and Wayne hurls a surprised O'Hara onto her bed before pushing off to confront McLaglen: "Danaher, you owe me three hundred and fifty pounds. Let's have it!" Danaher relents, but true to the Duke's rulebook, this is a question of honour, not finance. Wayne allows the money to be burned, O'Hara trots off home to make the supper, while Wayne and McLaglen enter history with one of cinema's most famous fist-fights. Wayne preserves his roughhouse charm and emerges victoriously to win his darling.

The Quiet Man was a resounding financial success in its day. Nominated for best picture in 1952, it was pipped at the post by director Cecil B DeMille's *The Greatest Show on Earth*, while Gary Cooper was crowned with the best actor award for his performance in the Fred Zinnemann western, *High Noon*.

Although the coveted Oscar statuette still eluded Wayne at this time, he was, however, a major box-office draw and the most popular American star during the 1950s. But his ultra-conservative views left some quarters unimpressed.

The 1952 espionage drama *Big Jim McLain* provided demonstrable proof of the Duke's political standpoint. Produced by the actor in tandem with Robert Fellows, and handled by *The Fighting Seabees* director Edward Ludwig, *Big Jim McLain* saw Big John in aggressive mood in the title role. The boisterous action sent the Duke to Hawaii, where he played an investigator of the House Un-American Activities Committee. His mission involved the flushing out of "commies", and the picture did not shy away from Wayne's personal belief system. Public and private persona were as one here, and *Big Jim McLain* remains – along with Wayne's gung-ho *The Green Berets* (1968) – a prime manifestation of the crusading Duke at his most belligerent. By the time the latter film went out to the American public, Wayne and the character that he portrayed on screen would be indistinguishable. Nevertheless, film fans back in 1953 could now revel in a better version of Wayne than *The Green Berets*.

"Big Jim McLain saw Big John in aggressive mood"

John Wayne as Big Jim McLain, a 1952 political
thriller with James Arness Hondo

he had to find her... he had to find...

WARNER BROS. PRESENT

THE C.V. WHITNEY PICTURE STARRING

JOHN WAYNE IN

"THE SEARCHERS"

THE STORY THAT SWEEPS FROM THE GREAT SOUTHWEST
TO THE CANADIAN BORDER IN

VistaVision
MOTION PICTURE HIGH FIDELITY

COLOR BY
TECHNICOLOR

JEFFREY HUNTER · VERA MILE
WARD BOND · NATALIE WOOD

SCREEN PLAY BY FRANK S. NUGENT   ASSOCIATE PRODUCER MERIAN C. COOPER   EXECUTIVE PRODUCER PATRIC

DIRECTED BY JOHN FORD   WARNE

THE BIGGEST,
ROUGHEST, TOUGHEST...
AND MOST BEAUTIFUL
PICTURE EVER MADE!

Every supreme film star is framed for eternity with at least one powerhouse incarnation. Deemed by Barry Norman to be "Simply the best western ever made," *The Searchers* stands the test of time and remains, for the Duke, the equivalent of other unbeatable displays: Marlon Brando's *On the Waterfront*, Robert De Niro's *The Godfather Part II*, Clint Eastwood's *The Outlaw Josey Wales*, Jack Nicholson's *Chinatown*, Larry Olivier's *Richard III* (or possibly *Henry V*) and Al Pacino's Scarface. This is not to say that such masters of the acting profession did not turn out other pieces of peerless work. Nevertheless, the timeless performance acts as a marker, and John Wayne marked his card in the role of Ethan Edwards. Before *The Searchers*, director John Ford had not made a western since concluding his cavalry trilogy with *Rio Grande* in 1950. With the burning desire to deliver a classic, Ford transplanted 250 cast and crew to shoot in the arid wastes of his adored Monument

Valley, Utah. Iconically, *The Searchers* opened in epic vein with Wayne's solitary figure riding into shot with the parched wilderness behind. Here was the complete anti-hero in the form of the Duke's mysterious Edwards, an ex-Confederate soldier draped in ambiguity. The trailer titles blazed proudly: "Adventure... from the sand-choked desert of Arizona to the snow-swept plains of Canada. Directed by John Ford in the breathtaking panorama of VistaVision." Wayne was presented heroically by the trailer itself: "From the thrilling pages of life rides a man you must fear and respect. A man whose unconquerable will and boundless determination carved a lusty, rough and boisterous slice of history called *The Searchers*. It's John Wayne as Ethan Edwards, who had a rare kind of courage, the courage that simply keeps on and on, far beyond all reasonable endurance..." The thrills ahead were laid out, and the drama was wound tightly.

The breathtaking scenery of
Monument Valley, Utah, 1956

For the uninitiated, the story is as follows: Ethan returns to the Monument Valley homestead of his brother, Aaron (Walter Coy), three years after the end of the American Civil War. He is in possession of a large amount of gold, and his post-war activities are a riddle, although it is explained that he did not show up to surrender. Ethan's former love, Martha (Dorothy Jordan), has married Aaron in the meantime. The pair have four children: teenagers Lucy and Ben (Pippa Scott and Robert Lyden), little Debbie (Lana Wood) and the adopted Martin Pawley (Jeffrey Hunter), whom Ethan rescued from Indian attack in the distant past but does not consider kin – Martin is eighth-Cherokee. Tragically, the happy peace of this family unit is shattered when a Comanche cattle raid diverts Ethan and an investigative group away from the dwelling. On their return, the men discover that Aaron, Aunt Martha and Ben have all been slaughtered, and their property torched. Both Lucy and young Debbie have been abducted by the Comanche chief, Scar (Henry Brandon).

"Simply the best western ever made"

Olive Carey, Jeffrey Hunter and Vira Miles in The Searchers

Henry Hathaway, Sophia Loren and John Wayne behind the scenes during filming of Legend of the Lost in 1957

ITALIAN ADVENTURE

FOLLOWING HIS CAREER-defining magnificence on *The Searchers*, Wayne was in the mood for travel in 1957, and trekked to Africa for the shooting of a fluffy piece of escapist exotica, *Legend of the Lost*. The film was co-produced with the involvement of the Duke's own production company, Batjac, and Henry Hathaway was in charge behind the camera. Before embarking with Wayne on location amongst the sandy expanses of the Libyan Sahara, the California-born director had squeezed a memorably unhinged turn out of debutant actor Richard Widmark – who would star alongside Wayne in 1960's *The Alamo* – as a giggling psychopath in *Kiss of Death* (1947). In addition, Hathaway had directed Marilyn Monroe in *Niagara* in 1953 – one of the ill-fated star's most interesting performances. Wayne would work in collaboration with Hathaway on various occasions after *Legend of the Lost*, the culmination of their outings together being Wayne's Oscar-winning star vehicle, *True Grit*, in 1969. Yet at this stage of his life, the Duke had to settle for implacable desert temperatures. Only slick sophisticate Rossano Brazzi and a blossoming goddess by name of

Sophia Loren were out there as company. It's lovely work if you can get it!

The shimmering heat of the far-off setting was captured by cinematographer Jack Cardiff. The British cameraman and occasional director is most famous for his Oscar-winning wonders on Michael Powell and Emeric Pressburger's rapturous *Black Narcissus* (1946), as well as their 1948 pearl, *The Red Shoes*. Later in his illustrious career, Cardiff would provide sterling service again in North Africa on director John Guillermin's all-star *Death on the Nile* (1978). It was on this glossy Agatha Christie adaptation that Cardiff was charged with bringing the ancient ruins to life – and that was just the cast! His industry paid off. Egypt smiled on triumphantly, and David Niven never looked so dapper.

Wayne cut an impressive dash himself in *Legend of the Lost*. He was in fine fettle for a man of 50, and led the line easily as desert guide Joe January in an appealing slice of hokum that concerned itself with the search for hidden treasure in a forgotten city. Brazzi was the scheming villain of the story, while Loren played the ravishing Dita, a slave girl with an

explosive temper. In her candid autobiography of 1979, the Italian bombshell offered perceptive insight about the overseas production and the Duke's incomparable charisma: "I was relieved to find that John Wayne was exactly as advertised. Big, authoritative, gruff but polite, and a pro through and through. He showed up right on the minute, knew all his lines and moves, worked hard all day long without letup, and quit right on the minute. There was no doubt that he was in command, the captain on the bridge of the ship. He did not have to exert his authority overtly because everyone automatically deferred to him." High praise, indeed, and the Latin superstar reminisced further in her book about the inevitability of her on-screen romance with Wayne: "Of course, after facing the rigors of sandstorms, tarantulas, rampaging natives, scorpions, thirst, heat, and a Brazzi gone mad, John and I fell into each other's arms as we were miraculously rescued by a desert caravan." As audiences reclined in darkened theatres all over the world in 1957, would they have wanted the ending any other way?

Sophia Loren and John Wayne in Legend of the Lost

On-screen attraction between John Wayne and Sophie Loren in
Legend of the Lost in 1957

John Wayne on the set of The Barbarian and the Geisha in 1958

The following year, Wayne disappeared to foreign climes once more, but the Duke's experience on *The Barbarian and the Geisha* (1958) could in no way compete with the exotic revelries of *Legend of the Lost*. Wayne now found himself under the direction of the mighty John Huston. The result was a clash of the titans, and proved to be the pair's one-and-only collaboration. As far as Wayne's performance went, he turned in a competent portrayal of Townsend Harris, a US Government envoy sent to the 'unknown' country of Japan for the purposes of a trade treaty. Nevertheless, the differences between director and star were enormous, and one can hardly imagine Wayne playing second fiddle to anyone. The Duke demonstrated the necessary strength of character and toughness in his role of distinguished statesman, but the passion was not there. Some people should just not work in partnership. Wayne would enjoy far more convivial company in his next screen outing with Howard Hawks.

Considered by some sectors of the critical community as the perfect western, 1959's *Rio Bravo* proved a tense, claustrophobic affair. The picture was shot largely indoors under the experienced eye of Hawks, and the situation at hand made the ideal stepping stone for the director's dissection of his key concerns.

The set-up of the film was simple, although that factor did in no way suggest a simplistic entertainment: good guys (and a very helpful good girl) would be pitted against bad guys, and the stresses of these individuals would then come under scrutiny in this environment. Radically different characters would have to pool their varied resources in order to vanquish their enemies. The group under pressure would constitute the developing plotline of the story, and the survival instinct within this friendly unit would be monitored. The small band that was bound together by trust and mutual necessity would be the object of close examination. However, the brewing storm of impending violence would have to be weathered by constant outbursts of humour, and lightened by the comedic interaction of the principal players. And what a collection they were!

Ricky Nelson and John Wayne in Rio Bravo, 1959

John Wayne and Angie Dickinson in Rio Bravo

Big John Wayne was the natural choice for leader of the pack as redoubtable sheriff, John T Chance. In the fear-inducing setting where the self-assured and self-reliant would emerge victoriously, Wayne was the embodiment of resolve, rising to defeat the forces of villainy with the help of cocky young gunslinger Ricky Nelson and two inadequate deputies. Splendid vintage character actor Walter Brennan played Stumpy, the semi-crippled jailhouse watchman, and an enthusiastic, pre-Rat Pack Dean Martin delivered an eye-opening performance as a soak eager to abandon the demon drink. Although outwardly in danger, this motley assortment of maleness would bond in adversity to overcome its assailants. As the female member of the crew – and definitely the brains – the delightful Angie Dickinson was the perfect contrast to Wayne's reliability in the guise of her nervy character, the garrulous Feathers. Talkaholic would be more to the point! Dickinson was on the road to success, for sure. The next year, she teamed up with Martin, Sinatra, Lawford and Bishop for director Lewis Milestone's *Ocean's Eleven*, decades before George Clooney and the boys thought it might be a good idea to rob a Las Vegas casino. Later, 1967 would pair Dickinson with occasional Wayne colleague Lee Marvin, in John Boorman's cult thriller, *Point Blank*. Painting and horror aficionados will also reserve a special place in their hearts for the blonde siren whenever they enter an art gallery… Film guru David Thomson is a major fan of Angie Dickinson, and obviously a gentleman of exquisite taste. His insightful comments about *Rio Bravo* gave typically perceptive praise to the Duke's massive star quality and organisational skills: "John Wayne watched over everyone like a football coach with rookies." Wayne was a great attraction at the time of *Rio Bravo*, and enjoyed a worldwide following. Someone was watching over the Duke, however. While on a visit to the United States in 1959, Soviet leader Nikita Krushchev had two particular objectives on his mind: firstly, to make a trip to Disneyland and, most urgently, to meet John Wayne. Glasnost, here we come.

"Big John Wayne was the natural leader of the pack"

John Wayne as Sheriff John T. Chance in Rio Bravo, 1959

John Wayne on the set of The Alamo in his dual role as director and actor in 1960

"Telling this tale proved a crusade for Wayne"

Alamo is Spanish for poplar tree, but the word has become associated with the eponymous Franciscan mission in Texas, defended courageously in 1836 by almost 200 idealistic 'Texicans' and freedom fighters. Desperate to gain independence from Mexico, the motley band became martyrs at the hands of Generalissimo Santa Anna's rampaging army. Wayne's titanic story opened proudly, yellow parchment standing on a grainy wood background. History was written in bold: "In the year of our Lord, 1836, Texas, which has known many flags, was then under the colors of Mexico. Though its inhabitants were made up of settlers from far countries and all parts of the United States, they were Mexican citizens all. Generalissimo Santa Anna was sweeping north across Mexico toward them, crushing all who opposed his tyrannical rule. They now faced the decision that all men in all times must face – the eternal choice of men – to endure oppression or to resist." Telling this tale proved a crusade for Wayne, and cinema trailers praised his toil: "It's here at last. The monumental, history-making motion picture fourteen years in the making. The $12-million epic, *The Alamo.*" Financial concerns aside, Wayne did not cut any corners in his quest for authenticity, either, while shooting. "Happy" Shahan engaged the help of a local construction wizard to fabricate a replica of the original mission. Big John was not convinced, and asked the Mexican maestro if he knew how to build. "Do you know how to make a movie, Mr Wayne?" came the amusing reply. The trio fell about for minutes! A friend of Shahan then lent 200 longhorn steers to complement the production's mighty appearance. 2,000 horses and riders took part in the explosive battle scenes, each man the proud owner of accurate period uniform. It all made for a great film experience, with the Duke's indomitable presence icing a wonderful cake.

The full cast from the epic movie The Alamo in 1960

Action scene from The Alamo

John Wayne directing a scene from The Alamo

The production was blessed before the cameras rolled, and Wayne was under terrific pressure. This was a massive undertaking, recalled by cinematographer William H Clothier: "It was a big job for Duke, there's no question about it. But he did it, and he did a good job. But I think he realised when it was over that it was too much, it wasn't worth it. Either direct the picture but don't act in it, or act and don't direct the picture." Actor Denver Pyle also explains the importance of Wayne to a film of such stature, and the classic Duke posture: "But nobody could play his big man. And [John] Ford taught him that. Ford taught him how to walk, how to move…" The ace director even provided his (uncredited) assistance on some of *The Alamo*'s exteriors, having shown up uninvited on the set, much to Wayne's irritation! This was a stressful time for the Duke as he juggled three roles. His character, Colonel Davy Crockett, was a typical emblem of courage, a beacon of hope for those brave few protecting Texas from the power of Generalissimo Santa Anna's encroaching army. Just like Sergeant Stryker in *Sands of Iwo Jima*, Crockett was a man overflowing with pride and an ideology that craved liberty at any cost.

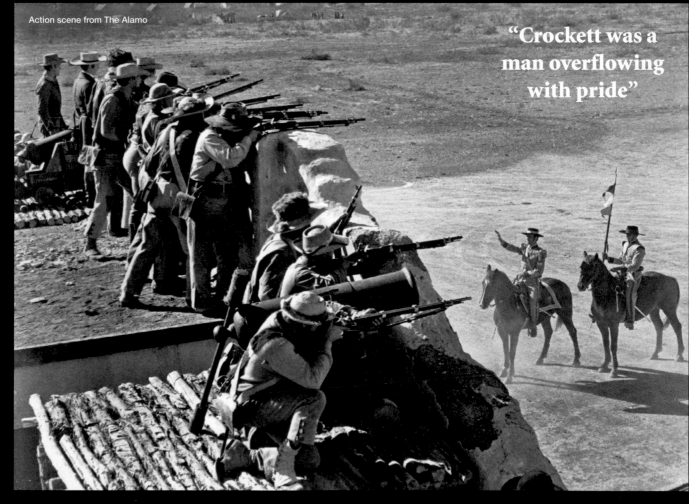
Action scene from The Alamo

"Crockett was a man overflowing with pride"

With the Tennessee hero as his mouthpiece, Wayne had the opportunity to expose his own values on film, and his political views were captured powerfully during Crockett's musings on the concept of Republic: "Republic. I like the sound of the word. It means people can live free, talk free, go or come, buy or sell, be drunk or sober, however they choose. Some words give you a feeling. Republic is one of those words that makes me tight in the throat. The same tightness a man gets when his baby takes his first step, or his first baby shaves and makes his first sound like a man. Some words can give you a feeling that makes your heart warm. Republic is one of those words." The statement packed a punch with its emotional endorsement of Wayne's ethos. This was a rousing speech on the nature of freedom that could be treated as a reinforcement of Wayne's unique vision. Crockett and the Duke would pursue honour to the death, and a revealing espousal of Wayne's moral code was on tap just before Crockett gallantly despatches Flaca (Linda Cristal) to safety: "There's right and there's wrong. You gotta do one or the other. You do the one and you're living. Do the other and you may be walking around, but you're dead as a beaver hat."

"Wayne had the opportunity to expose his own values on film"

John Wayne as Davy Crockett in The Alamo

John Wayne and his daughter on the set of The Comancheros, 1961

Magnanimously, and indicative of Wayne's benevolent nature, he insisted on receiving no screen credit for his contribution behind the camera. Cast-wise, the picture featured an appearance from lazy-eyed stalwart Jack Elam, playing a heavy. The one-time accountant and hotel manager would attain cult status with director Sergio Leone's *Once Upon a Time in the West* (1968), and would saddle up again with Big John in 1970's *Rio Lobo*. Wayne, naturally, was on solid form in *The Comancheros*, portraying Texas Ranger Captain Jake Cutter, a crafty individual who makes sensible use of the gambler he has taken in on a firearms offence. Handsome co-star Stuart Whitman brought his indisputable charm to the good-natured proceedings with his character of Paul Regret, and would do battle alongside Wayne the following year in *The Longest Day*. An admirable piece of work from all concerned, *The Comancheros* also benefited from a typically rousing Elmer Bernstein score and featured panoramic vistas of Arizona and Utah.

"Hatari! was gaudy, escapist entertainment of the highest order"

Hardy Kruger, Elsa Martinelli, John Wayne, Red Buttons, Valentin de Vargas and Michele Girardon on the set of Harari! in 1962

1962 proved a year of exciting travel for Wayne as he packed his suitcase for Africa. Hatari! saw Wayne the adventurer trekking off again with old-hand director Howard Hawks. On this occasion, the colourful production cast the Duke in the role of Sean Mercer, a hardy big-game hunter capturing animals on the savannah for subsequent sale to circuses and zoos. Hatari! was gaudy, escapist entertainment of the highest order. Popular with audiences, a whale of a time was also had by cast and crew in this faraway excuse for a holiday.

Also in 1962, Wayne starred in one of his most critically acclaimed westerns, The Man Who Shot Liberty Valance. Directed by American-born poet, John Ford, the atmospheric period piece stood up as an elegiac, bittersweet tribute to the Old West, a lost, bygone world where the bullet would be substituted, inevitably, by the ballot box as the weapon of choice. Myth would coagulate with reality in

Ford's contemplative analysis of the collision between past and present, and the look of the era was realised by costume designer Edith Head – a regular servant of the great Alfred Hitchcock – and Hal Pereira's gloomy art direction. The gifted duo would add their creative expertise to Wayne's El Dorado in 1967. As The Man Who Shot Liberty Valance opens with a sense of grief, proud Senator Ransom Stoddard (James Stewart) has returned in the 'future' of 1910 to the western town of Shinbone with his wife, Hallie (Vera Miles). They have come to pay their respects at the funeral of Stoddard's old friend, Tom Doniphon (John Wayne). Years earlier, Stoddard had travelled to the frontier outpost as an ambitious, idealistic lawyer. Lending his charismatic, experienced support to the movie as a man of learning later elected to the US Senate, accomplished actor Stewart produced another powerful performance.

Without doubt, the picture became one of John Wayne's most popular films. It was received enthusiastically by the American public in its day – playing in some theatres for several weeks – and confirmed the Duke's infectious charm and magnificent stature with his portrayal of the respected cattle baron of the title. A tower of a performer, Wayne dominates the frame in his scenes, even when facing fierce opposition from tempestuous co-star Maureen O'Hara, an actress with whom he enjoyed a warm rapport and fizzing screen chemistry. In *McLintock!*, Wayne's character wins out finally, in no small part thanks to his ability to take matters in hand, and his instantly likeable manner. Cinema advertising of the time hailed the movie and main man loudly: "*McLintock* is McNificent!" Leading lady Maureen O'Hara was promoted before expectant audiences as "an irresistible firebrand of a redhead." The mighty teasers were confirmed by healthy box-office returns. The film was a monster hit in 1963, validation of Wayne's desire to take the western off in a fresh direction after his previous excursions into the genre had been more thoughtful. *McLintock!* also established the Duke, again, as one of the year's most commanding stars.

Well into his fifties by now, Wayne was always the accomplished lead, but his hard-won experience and elevated position in the film fraternity allowed him to send up his own image and introduce endearing touches of self-parody into his work. *McLintock!* was a boisterous, no-holds-barred affair, and its iconic mudhole brawl was immortalised on screen by stunt supremo and respected fight co-ordinator Cliff Lyons. Wayne had always played it harder than hard when necessary, and the opportunity for a fight was never amiss. Equivocal chief protagonist George Washington McLintock was not a man to cross, but the Duke was still affable – to a point – when pushed: "I'm gonna use good judgement. I haven't lost my temper in forty years, but Pilgrim, you caused a lotta trouble this morning, mighta got somebody killed, and somebody oughta belt you in the mouth. But I won't. I won't. The hell I won't!" Chaos ensues!

Filmed mainly in Tucson, Arizona, the production was immensely enjoyable for cast and crew alike, but never at the public's expense. Wayne was far too savvy to topple into the sticky trap that frequently curses comedy. The larger-than-life entertainment on display in *McLintock!* can be seen as a variation of sorts on *Taming of the Shrew*, and Wayne brought his megastar status to the knockabout movie for all the family. The combined ingredients proved a sure-fire winner for a smash. Brawling, domestic strife and constant doses of good humour ensured that the proceedings went by at a fair old clip. As the female star in the challenging role of Big John's irascible wife, Katherine, the always-lovely Maureen O'Hara submitted gamely to a host of indignities – all heaped upon her with audience satisfaction in mind. O'Hara found herself caked from head to toe in mud and endured a thick molasses drenching in the best spirits.

Maureen O'Hara and John Wayne in McLintock!, 1963

"McLintock! was one of Wayne's most popular films"

"Brawling, domestic strife and constant doses of good humour"

John Wayne and Maureen O'Hara get a laugh out of their muddied state on location of McLintock!, 1963

"A worthy endeavour of truly epic proportions"

John Wayne in 'The Magnificent Showman'
also known as Circus World in 1964

Rita Hayworth and John Wayne in The Magnificent Showman, 1964

Although he was apparently indestructible at this lofty moment in his career, Wayne was found to have cancer in 1964. In never-say-die fashion, however, the Duke took a break from the film world after the making of *McLintock!*, and then conquered his illness. Admittedly, he had to have ribs and a lung removed, but it was no surprise to see this colossal individual soldiering on determinedly with his life and work. That same year of 1964, the unbreakable Wayne was back on screen with the mighty circus drama, *The Magnificent Showman*. This was a production originally meant for director Frank Capra, the master of emotion, but action stalwart Henry Hathaway was the eventual choice. Conforming to trends of the period that made the shooting of pictures in Europe far more cost effective for American studios, cast and crew

set off for Madrid. The Spanish capital seemed a perfect locale when considering the Duke's fiery female support. Latin temptress Rita Hayworth added her glossy attributes to the proceedings in her role as Wayne's ex-wife, while burgeoning Italian star Claudia Cardinale turned the dramatics into a battle of the beauties as the Duke's daughter. In contrast to the excessive glamour, Wayne brought a hard-nosed edge to his character of Matt Masters, a tough circus proprietor faced with problems in and out of the Big Top. The tawdry charm and heady excitement of this sawdust world had often wowed cinema crowds. One only has to call to mind movies such as *Freaks, The Greatest Show on Earth* and *Trapeze* to conjure up the atmosphere. *The Magnificent Showman* was a fine addition to the circus canon, and

Wayne then moved on into biblical territory.

The life and times of Jesus Christ have seen a myriad of screen incarnations, and the 1965 extravaganza, *The Greatest Story Ever Told*, was an enormous excursion into familiar territory. The tale should need no introduction, but to paraphrase the great Oscar Wilde: "Do go on, I'm so desperate to know what happens!" A reverential account of Christ's existence on Earth, *The Greatest Story Ever Told* still retains the questionable honour of being one of the most lengthy motion pictures ever made. There are many versions about, several of which have been truncated for broadcast on television, but the original ran at well over four hours. This was a worthy endeavour of truly epic proportions, with the sandy wastes of Utah doubling for the

Palestinian setting in days of yore. An A-list, all-star cast was an unavoidable requirement of a film of such magnitude, and Max von Sydow turned in a compelling performance as Jesus Christ. Telly Savalas made for an intriguing Pontius Pilate, while biblical giant Charlton Heston brought depth to his part as the tragic John the Baptist. Yet the most inspirational piece of casting, in my opinion, was to have the Duke in the role of the centurion at Christ's crucifixion. Although Wayne's display was not to everyone's taste and little more than a glorified cameo, Big John was an admirable choice, and his contribution to the movie is preserved with the often-quoted line: "Truly this man was the son of God." Gravitas was the necessary quality here, and Big John was the man to provide it.

Objectively, *The Green Berets* is a long haul, even if you must have grasped by now that I reserve considerable admiration and affection for Big John. The opening segment at the American training camp certainly proceeds at a *more* than leisurely pace. This is where the Duke makes initial contact with cynical journalist George Beckworth (David Janssen), a character whose views of the conflict will be altered through consistent exposure to bloodshed. Providing a modicum of balance with his part, Janssen was most famous for his role as Dr Richard Kimble in the smash-hit 1960s' TV series *The Fugitive*, and takes off with the Duke on his assignment into enemy territory. Once Wayne's grizzled character Colonel Mike Kirby arrives at the front in South Vietnam, however, affairs definitely hot up, and there are some respectable action sequences, not least the impressive moments that introduce a flurry of helicopters. The movie must have been a monumental administrative undertaking for all. President at the time, Lyndon B Johnson is said to have offered unanimous support to the Duke, as a result of the actor's written request for assistance with his venture. In the necessary pursuit of authenticity, no logistic expense was spared by the Pentagon as far as equipment, advice and military personnel were concerned. Nevertheless, the film seems

extraordinarily clunky by today's standards. The blood gleams with that familiar shine of 1960s' ketchup; a camp populated by Viet Cong forces is riddled in a sudden attack with sprays of machine-gun fire, and a whole regiment of extras tumbles in synchronised unison like dominoes; as a bridge explodes in another momentous scene, top stuntmen demonstrate their finest displays of diving as their bodies leap like salmon into the air. This is cartoon warfare of the most unsophisticated kind, and although I do not in any way subscribe to the politics – and reasons – that propelled the campaign in Vietnam, I cannot fault Wayne for his total immersion in a subject that was undoubtedly close to his heart. *The Green Berets* is a movie – in many ways more of an 'experience' than a movie – that has engendered endless reams of enraged invective about Wayne and his right-wing political persuasion from commentators. A product of both its time and star, the picture is certainly an extreme piece of propaganda in defence of the American cause, and segments of enthusiastic action do not compensate for the film's unavoidable longueurs. Be that as it may, and accepting that *The Green Berets* does not warrant my inclusion even as a guilty pleasure within the Wayne canon, I would hope, at least, that its snaking queues of detractors have actually bothered to watch it.

Edward Faulkner, John Wayne and George Takei

"In the necessary pursuit of authenticity, no logistic expense was spared"

"An extreme piece of propaganda in defence of the American cause"

Epic battle scenes typified John Wayne's Vietnam War movie The Green Berets

Scene from John Wayne's anti-communist depiction of the Vietnam War, The Green Berets

Production shot from the acclaimed western True Grit directed by Henry Hathaway, 1969

George Sherman and John Wayne in Big Jake
directed by George Sherman

Chris Mitchum stayed with Wayne again for the 1971 western, *Big Jake*. The picture was in many ways a star vehicle for the Duke, and a nostalgic farewell on at least two counts. Earlier in his lengthy and accomplished career, veteran *Big Jake* director George Sherman had enjoyed employment at a variety of studios from the mid 1930s onwards, and had even handled a pre-stardom Wayne in some of the *Three Mesquiteers* series. In an admirable gesture of respect and by means of acknowledging this debt, Wayne revealed his much-trumpeted loyalty by honouring Sherman's previous service and asking him in person to direct the movie. Sherman had spent most of the 1960s working behind the cameras for television, and one can assume that he was only too delighted to be called up by the Duke for his final feature film. With *Big Jake*, Wayne said a fond goodbye to iridescent screen partner Maureen O'Hara as well. This amusing outing proved to be the pair's final screen collaboration, and the end of a magnificent partnership. In the story, O'Hara played along as Martha to Wayne's Jacob "Jake" McCandles, and in customary style for this latter period of his working life, the Duke was in no way afraid to make fun of himself and his macho image. Wayne's son, Patrick, displayed a touch of youthful exuberance in the acting department, and the enjoyable exercise displayed the commendably engaging chemistry of father and son together.

"The Duke was in no way afraid to make fun of himself and his macho image"

John Wayne as Jacob McCandles in Big Jake, 1971

Directed by Mark Rydell, Wayne's 1972 western, *The Cowboys*, addressed the gloomy theme of vengeance, and was certainly no favourite with critical opinion of its day. Vigilantism as film subject matter had reared its grisly head only the previous year with director Don Siegel's violent police thriller, *Dirty Harry*. The established star of that controversial picture was gritty actor Clint Eastwood, a hero who brought all his jaded cynicism and low-key technique to the table in the role of Inspector "Dirty" Harry Callahan. Commentators of the period had gushed with a torrent of hysteria in their condemnation of Callahan's brutal retribution. Yet here was a cop not "Dirty" in his approach but the recipient of all the dirty jobs that no-one else was man enough to take – in this case tracking down a vicious serial killer preying on San Francisco.

Without wishing to force the comparison too far, *The Cowboys* rode off into similar territory. This was a poignant picture remembered fondly by Wayne connoisseurs for the Duke's emotional depiction of a veteran rancher, forced by circumstance into engaging the services of a young bunch of boys. Wayne was reliably solid in this nuanced, father-figure role of Wil Andersen. What are the other options when deserted by his hired help? Also, what are the choices available to this greenhorn group of hands when their kind mentor, Andersen, falls victim to dastardly villain Bruce Dern? The latter's effective portrayal of the baddie, Long Hair, establishes the ancient western struggle between good and evil. Dern is the killer on the loose, and the coming-of-age story revolves around the action chosen by the cowboys of the title. These are lads destined to grow into men by combative confrontation, and although the message on offer was pilloried savagely by writers at the time, how can you not sanction the avenging of John Wayne in a western setting? The justification of violent revenge plays out naturally in *The Cowboys*. Peaceful reaction would be out of keeping with the world it depicts. As an analogy, imagine a Mafia movie where venerated local mobster Robert De Niro is gunned down right in front of his neighbourhood acolytes. Would these teenage protégés disappear home sheepishly to mamma or take *vendetta* into their own hands? I rest my case.

"The Cowboys was a poignant picture remembered fondly by Wayne connoisseurs"

Mark Rydell, John Ford and John Wayne on the set of The Cowboys, 1972

JOHN WAYNE

IS

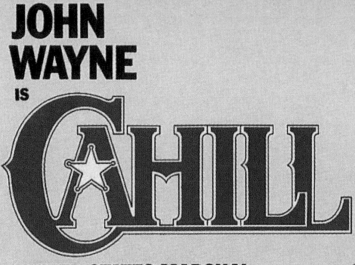

CAHILL

UNITED STATES MARSHAL

Break the law and he's the <u>last</u> man you want to see.

And the <u>last</u> you ever will.

JOHN WAYNE in A BATJAC PRODUCTION
"CAHILL: UNITED STATES MARSHAL"
Also Starring GARY GRIMES · NEVILLE BRAND and
GEORGE KENNEDY as Fraser
Screenplay by HARRY JULIAN FINK and RITA M. FINK

In 1973, Wayne stepped back with typical panache onto far less problematic ground than *The Cowboys*. The Duke now found himself on familiar terrain, with the Batjac-produced entertainment entitled *The Train Robbers*. Director Burt Kennedy of *The War Wagon* fame brought his penchant for boisterous action to the proceedings, and the publicity posters were quick to explain the dynamics of the story: "The gold or the grave. The young widow could lead them to either." In this enjoyable, uncomplicated yarn, Wayne was entrusted with representing the gruff Lane, and waltzed through the adventure without any difficulty. Although just over the age of retirement, Wayne was charisma personified. He had admitted to respectful journalists that he was no longer in line to portray "those young lieutenants any more," but his last few roles on the screen revealed a master at work whose advanced years contributed both charm and profundity to character. Lane was a man hired by the lovely Ann-Margret's shamed widow, Mrs Lowe, to locate the loot that her late husband had purloined – and thereby restore her reputation. Without doubt, The Duke had always relished a job like this, and took to his assignment with distinction.

1973's *Cahill – United States Marshal* gave extra endorsement to Wayne's identity, and also to his uncontested credibility. Batjac publicity posters trailed the star as a frightening hero: "Break the law and he's the last man you want to see. And the last you ever will." In the same manner that Pierce Brosnan's 007 proved authentic as an icy assassin over 20 years later, Wayne would always make a believable figure on screen. Directed by Andrew V McLaglen, *Cahill* gave the ageing Duke free rein to demonstrate his paternal instincts in the title role. Wayne portrayed JD Cahill, a hard-toiling westerner whose two teenage boys – victims of their father's neglect – have been taken under the ill-advised wing of local outlaw Abe Fraser (George Kennedy). True to form, the Duke confronts the felon, and law and order are restored for the benefit of all. Along for this moralistic ride was *film noir* favourite Marie Windsor (*The Narrow Margin*), who added her signature touch of class to the production.

As Wayne's life on the screen began to ebb away slowly, 1974 witnessed the first of two police procedurals for the Duke in as many years. In *McQ*, a cult favourite from *The Magnificent Seven* director John Sturges, Wayne was in suitably embittered mode as Seattle-based detective Lieutenant Lon McQ, a determined individual who refused to take 'no' for an answer while looking into the death of a close buddy. Former editor and action specialist Sturges had thrilled children of all ages at the cinema years before *McQ*. *Bad Day at Black Rock* had made for a brooding, atmospheric western with reliable old hands Spencer Tracy and Robert Ryan, while the major Second World War movie by name of *The Great Escape* should need no introduction. Even Clint Eastwood had succumbed to the lure of the respected Sturges with his lesser-known western from 1972, *Joe Kidd*. In the same year that saw the release of *McQ*, Wayne also made a memorably fun visit to Harvard University. Invited to this great seat of American learning, the Duke made an imposing entrance, riding heroically into the expectant campus perched on top of an armoured personnel carrier. Great men will always reveal their greatness through great actions, and here was the perfect example. Wayne was on site as an honorary guest, and the prize to collect was the aptly named Brass Balls award. Could there have been a worthier recipient of such a distinguished laurel? A rowdy question-and-answer session added to the entertainment on the day's line-up, and the Duke was quick to demonstrate his typically assured sense of humour when put on the spot suddenly about his appearance: "That's real hair. Not mine, but real hair!" High-spirited undergraduates were no match for Wayne.

A scene from John Sturges' crime drama McQ, 1974

"True to form, the Duke confronts the felon, and law and order are restored"

John Wayne as Lane in The Train Robbers, a 1973 western
written and directed by Burt Kennedy

Wayne followed up the tough police thriller *McQ* with *Brannigan* in 1975, a romping crime picture set on the streets of London town. British director Douglas Hickox took up position behind the lens for the Batjac production, and had cut his teeth with experience in the world of commercials. Prior to working on *Brannigan*, Hickox's two most acclaimed features had taken him into the murky depths of black comedy. *Entertaining Mr Sloane* (1969) had proved a colourful transposition from board to screen of Joe Orton's popular stage play, while the cult 1973 horror film, *Theatre of Blood*, had ushered a performance of vintage camp out of the incomparable Vincent Price. With its inventive methods of slaughter derived from the gory plots of Shakespearean dramas – and visited by Price's ham actor on his dismissive critics – *Theatre of Blood* was enormously entertaining, and remains a favoured old friend of horror aficionados to this day. With Hickox, the Duke was on wonderful form for *Brannigan*, remaining businesslike and presentably suave on any occasion – even without a tie! In this loose variation on the modern western *Coogan's Bluff* from director Don Siegel – the man entrusted with helming the Duke's final picture one year later – Wayne made for a typically endearing star as Jim Brannigan, an experienced US policeman jetting into the capital to apprehend gangster-on-the-run John Vernon. In his sympathetic supporting depiction of Scotland Yard head honcho, Commander Swann, Dickie Attenborough had the unenviable responsibility of monitoring Big John's behaviour – and dress code – and this meeting of two diametrically opposed cultures (and accents) made for the most intriguing partnership. Actresses Lesley-Anne Down and the always-alluring Judy Geeson provided the movie's beauty, and the action-packed spectacle was complemented by a whistle-stop parade of glamorous London locations – with forgiveness heaped by an enthusiastic audience on the occasionally skewed geography! A welcome shot of the Albert Memorial and a thrilling car chase were thrown into the glossy mix, making *Brannigan* an uncomplicated and exemplary last appearance by the Duke on English soil.

Wayne continued the distinguished approach with his penultimate western in 1975. In director Stuart Millar's *Rooster Cogburn*, the Duke was catapulted back into well-known *True Grit* territory, where he rode on in the formidable guise of Reuben J Rooster Cogburn. Here was heroic toughness coupled with a touching tale outdoors.

Relieved of his marshal's status in the movie, Wayne had to merit the return of his badge the hard way, by rounding up a group of thieving outlaws. The Duke's quest was complicated on another level by the arrival of uncompromising old buzzard Katharine Hepburn – in a hectoring, Bible-bashing role that invited comparison with her fondly remembered part of Rose Sayer in director John Huston's *The African Queen* (1951). All in a day's work on the range, Wayne found himself required to saddle up for the added mission of tracking down the murderers of the lady's father. A rousing picture with many qualities, *Rooster Cogburn* made for a fascinating battle of the sexes. This is where the paragons of machismo and feminism met head to head, and the eager confrontation of two great stars was the end product. The partnership between Wayne and Hepburn intrigued audiences, and confirmed that the Duke could hold his own effortlessly in the regal company of one of Hollywood's most adored – and accomplished – leading ladies. No mean feat.

"The partnership between Wayne and Hepburn intrigued audiences"

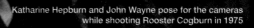

Katharine Hepburn and John Wayne pose for the cameras while shooting Rooster Cogburn in 1975

"The Duke was in wonderful form for Brannigan"

The 1975 British action film Brannigan starring John Wayne, a Chicago detective sent to London to organise the extradition of an American mobster (John Vernon)

John Wayne in his last ever film The Shootist in 1976. Wayne plays ageing gunfighter, John Bernard Books

John Wayne and Lauren Bacall
in The Shootist, 1976

FINAL BOW

THE MOVIE LIFE of every superlative performer has to come to an end, and it was no surprise to discover that Wayne's last cinematic outing was a western. With director Don Siegel's *The Shootist* in 1976, the myth of the great John Wayne was set in stone. The Duke's farewell appearance on the silver screen, this magnificent fusion of reality and legend proved a touching swansong to a titanic career. Tender tribute was paid to Wayne during the opening montage of *The Shootist*'s reverential title sequence, a selection of clips recognising the Duke's unforgettable contribution to the western, while subtly introducing his character within the film. In his portrait of seasoned gunslinger John Bernard Books, Wayne presented a mirror image of himself and a performance of rare depth. As a hymn to the heroes and atmosphere of the Old West from Siegel, *The Shootist* allowed Wayne – the western's leading light – to bid farewell on a majestic note. The story unfolded at the dawn of the 20th century, a time of change in Carson City, Nevada. 1901 saw the inevitable march of civilisation replacing the old staples of horse and gun, yet the lofty moral code of Books had timeless value: "I won't be wronged, I won't be insulted, and I won't be laid a hand on. I don't do these things to other people and I expect the same from them." Wayne rode gracefully into town with this credo on his lips, and took up lodgings with spirited widow, *Bond Rogers* – portrayed perfectly by film aristocracy Lauren Bacall. Rogers was a landlady, and her impressionable young son was played by Ron Howard – a face already familiar to 1970s' TV audiences for his part as Richie Cunningham in the sitcom *Happy Days*, with Henry Winkler's smooth-as-velvet Fonz for company. Howard's role of wide-eyed

youngster Gillom recalled Brandon de Wilde's hero-worshipping turn in *Shane*. Later in his career, Howard would morph into a successful Hollywood director. The 1995 Tom Hanks space saga *Apollo 13* is one notable example.

A rich visual experience, *The Shootist* was filmed lovingly in Technicolor by Dirty Harry cinematographer Bruce Surtees. Top-notch director Don Siegel had previously travelled to western terrain on two Clint Eastwood pictures – *Two Mules for Sister Sara* (1970) and *The Beguiled* (1971) – while his work immediately prior to *The Shootist* had seen him twice in thriller mode. 1973's cult movie *Charley Varrick* had pitted Walter Matthau against the Mob, while *The Black Windmill* (1974) featured Michael Caine alongside the ever-lovely Delphine Seyrig. *The Magnificent Seven*'s musical supremo Elmer Bernstein confirmed the undeniable quality on show in Siegel's drama and *Stagecoach* co-star John Carradine appeared in the line-up, as well, a distinct reminder of Wayne's superstar beginnings. Sometimes, everything returns naturally to the starting point. Memories of 1939 fluttered softly like butterflies, but Wayne's character, Books – and the Duke himself – were carrying an impossible load. Confronted by the stern presence of Lauren Bacall's landlady, Bond Rogers – making bread busily in her kitchen – Wayne's ageing character is told in no uncertain terms to vacate the premises, having apparently duped the widow into thinking that he possessed unimpeachable credentials: "You lied to me," accuses Rogers, "you made a fool out of me and you took advantage of me. This house is all I have and if my lodgers find out who you are, they'll leave."

Wayne's interjection is unsettlingly honest: "I have a cancer. I'm dying of it." If the world was uncertain about Wayne's private circumstances at this time – although the plight of such an enormous star and his well-publicised stomach cancer must have been common knowledge – this was the moment when the Duke stepped from the screen and entered our hearts for eternity. Wayne and his character were interchangeable at this point, even though they already had been on many occasions, yet the compelling drama played out from here with all the tragedy and emotions of real life. Wayne would star in cancer-research advertisements on American television around the time of *The Shootist*, and the commercials would include the scene in which Books is himself diagnosed by the James Stewart character, Doctor Hostetler. This was proof positive of Wayne's desire to raise awareness of the disease, and testament to the man's altruistic nature. In the film, the Duke's

admission of his condition resulted in a tender friendship between Books and Rogers. Interviewed by movie expert and enthusiastic critic, Mark Cousins, in 2000, Bacall was remarkably candid about her rapport on screen with Big John – and with the actor off camera – admitting that "...we not only got along well, but we were

attracted to one another." Having laughed about Wayne's tendency to take control of scenes with typical authority, and his love of instruction on set, Bacall adds: "But we really got along incredibly well. The chemistry was really good." Acceptance indeed of Wayne's bewitching personal magnetism. Yet who could not have got along incredibly well with John Wayne, even if one accepts his dominant personality and considerable contradictions? An individual blessed with all the gifts and charisma of the Duke can only inspire respectful admiration. As for Books, he was cut from the same heroic cloth as Wayne, and decided finally to exit life in a blaze of glory against three cocky young gunmen rather than succumb to the protracted horrors of terminal illness. A saloon confrontation beckoned the Duke appropriately before his final curtain, and for those of you who have not yet experienced *The Shootist*, the ending awaits you patiently.

Lauren Bacall and John Wayne during the filming of The Shootist

"The Duke stepped from the screen and entered our hearts for eternity"

SUNDOWN

"Age, heart disease and cancer began to take their cruel, deadly toll"

Campaigning with President Gerald Ford in Orange County, CA, late in 1976

AS JOHN WAYNE hung up his hat and spurs and tethered his horse outside the saloon at the close of the most majestic screen career, age, heart disease and cancer began to take their cruel, deadly toll on the actor during the ultimate years of his life. However immortal all great men might seem, they can only continue for so long. Wayne was a late convert to Catholicism near the end, possibly as a source of solace in the face of the inevitable. He was remarkably open in a famous television interview with journalist Barbara Walters in 1979, and talked emotionally about his situation and the spirituality that guided his day-to-day activity. In a manner that spoke volumes about his fortitude and profundity, Wayne was typically amusing when explaining his belief system to Walters: "I spoke to the Man up there on many occasions… but I've always had deep faith that there is a supreme being. There has to be. You know, it's just… to me it's just a normal thing to have that kind of faith. The fact that He's let me stick around a little longer – or She's let me stick around a little longer! – certainly goes great with me, and I wanna hang around as long as I'm healthy and not in anybody's way." Sadly, the magnificent Duke was far from healthy at the time, and it reveals an admirable level of humility within Wayne to assume that he might have been a burden.

John Wayne is hugged by Sammy Davis Jr. with Yul Brynner, Johnny Carson, Shirley Jones and others at the end of the Academy Awards ceremony in 1979

"Wayne received a standing ovation from the audience, and was visibly moved"

America and the world warmed to the dying star, of course, and were universally sympathetic to the faltering Duke's plight in 1979. It was heartbreaking for the faithful to witness the ravages of cancer on the macho, patriotic warrior of *The Alamo* and *The Longest Day*. Having endured major valve surgery on his heart in early 1978, Wayne had received 150,000 messages of goodwill in only two months from an adoring, loyal public. Like our friends, we know deep down who our true stars are, and this iconic legend of the movies and life was now on the verge of taking one final, distinguished bow. As John Wayne walked down the steps to present Michael Cimino's *The Deer Hunter* with the Oscar for best picture at the Academy Awards spectacular in April 1979, it was a truly emotional occasion. Fittingly, Wayne received a standing ovation from the audience, and was visibly moved. He had lost a considerable amount of weight as the pains of disease ran amok, but he still cut a distinguished figure in

his tuxedo. What a rare, heart-warming sight it was to see John Wayne taken by surprise, with a tear in his eye. Far more importantly, though – and impossible to accept for anyone who had spent time in the Duke's company either on or off screen – was the thought that John Wayne would soon be no more. John Wayne, this rugged jewel of a man, and a superstar who had shone for so long with such splendour, was soon to depart from life and ride away into a celestial sunset.

The UCLA Medical Center in Los Angeles proved to be the last call for the Duke. Just over 30 years on, the facility would play host to unprecedented displays of public sorrow in response to the sudden demise of a musical great. This is where 'King of Pop' Michael Jackson would be pronounced dead in June 2009, following a suspected cardiac arrest. Although positioned at polar opposites of the entertainment spectrum, Wayne and Jackson were celebrities with a worldwide fan base, and different generations would mourn their loss.

"The Duke lives among those of us who so wish it"

John Wayne passed away on 11th June 1979, just weeks after the occasion of his 72nd birthday. One would hope that his illustrious spirit rose up to take the shape of a star in the sky. An elevated position in the firmament, looking over the parched wilderness of Utah's Monument Valley, would constitute a fitting place of rest and perpetual brightness for the Duke. Or the lone sands of Iwo Jima, or the twinkling green vales of Ireland. The choice is endless, and there is no correct answer. The solutions to this particular guessing game are many. The Duke lives among those of us who so wish it. His performances endure, even several decades after being committed to film. Wayne's contribution to the world of cinema was gigantic, and his seat among the pantheon of movie titans is assured. He was not the greatest actor of all, admittedly. It would be a Herculean task for anyone to compete in front of the camera with the talent of Marlon Brando. However, if you desire the heady concoction of consistent popularity combined with dashes of sheer manliness and charisma in spades – shaken with a final measure of grit and unpredictability – then I will give you John Wayne towering head and shoulders above all. My favourite five actors of the screen, in the fairest order of the lot – alphabetical – would have to be Robert De Niro, Clint Eastwood, Larry Olivier ("Don't snivel!"), Al Pacino and John Wayne. Although the Duke could not match the uncoiled venom of De Niro, the laid-back humour of Eastwood, the theatrical pedigree of Olivier, or even the eye-rolling fireworks of Pacino, I will settle for Wayne as my male choice on account of the following: total domination of the screen in all of his stellar performances; romantic appeal – albeit in the manner of an unpolished diamond – courage; character; the uniquely undervalued legacy of patriotism; charm, and a voice to tame the desert. John Wayne. Number one. Inimitable.

John Wayne on the set of Chisum in 1970. Wayne played a virtuous, ranch-owning patriarch who stopped a nothing to get control of the trade in Lincoln County

John Wayne as "Rooster" Cogburn in True Grit, 1969

Wayne was honoured at his funeral with one of his favourite pieces of music. Dimitri Tiomkin's Oscar-winning score from the 1954 disaster picture *The High and the Mighty* rang out. The lofty strains soared loudly, as they paid worthy tribute to the passing of a legend. May the Duke rest in eternal peace.

Shortly before Wayne's death, President Jimmy Carter had conferred on him the Congressional Medal of Honour. Maureen O'Hara had tabled the idea to Congress, with backing from several Wayne co-stars, including Kirk Douglas, Katharine Hepburn and Robert Stack. Such weighty pillars of Hollywood all vouched for Wayne's suitability. Replicas of the award were printed *en masse* to be worn by the grieving citizens of America. The inscription proclaimed with pride: "John Wayne, American." In 1980, Wayne was granted the top accolade available to American citizens: the Presidential Medal of Freedom.

"They paid worthy tribute to the passing of a legend"

John Wayne on the set of The Man Who Shot Liberty Valance, 1962

THE DUKE RIDES ON

AS THE ENDURING symbol of all things American, a combination of the never-say-die qualities of compassion and righteousness, Wayne enjoys continuing popularity and remains a source of inspiration to many. He is a regular entry in the Harris Poll for America's favourite screen stars, while The John Wayne Cancer Institute in Santa Monica, California – initiated in the early 1980s by The Wayne Foundation with loyal son Michael at the head – provides a sense of determination and resilience for those aiming to defeat the disease. Bravery was a key component of Wayne's fabric, and he would surely have welcomed the specialised varieties of research and education that the organisation offers.

Wayne had originally planned to have the following epitaph on his tombstone, a humble acknowledgement of how he saw himself: "Feo, fuerte y formal." ("Ugly, strong and distinguished.") I can agree with the latter two adjectives, but not with the first, which presents Wayne at his most self-critical. Let it be remembered that Wayne was married on three occasions in life – to attractive women of Latin-American origin, and he undoubtedly enjoyed the attentions of the ladies. First wife Josephine Alicia Saenz bore Wayne two boys and two girls between 1934 and 1940: Michael, Patrick, Toni and Melinda. The union ended in divorce in 1945. Fiery Mexican actress Esperanza Baur stayed with the Duke from 1946 to 1954, while third

spouse Pilar Pallete stood alongside Wayne from 1954 until his demise, the proud mother of Ethan – named after the Duke's iconic hero in *The Searchers* – and also two daughters, Aissa and Marisa. Wayne is alleged to have had affairs, too, maybe with none other than the alluring Marlene Dietrich. In addition, an examination of the Wayne roster of female co-stars reveals an endless list of beauties: to recall a few, actresses such as Janet Leigh, Maureen O'Hara, Sophia Loren, Angie Dickinson, Rita Hayworth, Elsa Martinelli, Claudia Cardinale and Yvonne De Carlo all added glamour to the Wayne mix. I would contend that he was by no means ugly, even if he chose to view himself this way with characteristic good humour.

John Wayne holds his daughter, Aissa, on the set of The Alamo, 1960

John Wayne as the infamous gunslinger Cole Thornton
and Johnny Crawford as Luke McDonald in El Dorado, 1967

"The most monumental star the silver screen has seen"

The actual inscription on the Wayne headstone passes better judgement than that which the great Duke would have desired for himself. The resting-place of one of America's most famous ambassadors can be found at Pacific View Memorial Park, Corona del Mar, in California's Orange County. Flowers sit quietly before the monument, which itself lies on the burnished grass. Simple at first, the centred capital letters on the grave take on a myriad of meanings:

"TOMORROW IS THE MOST
IMPORTANT THING IN LIFE.
COMES INTO US AT MIDNIGHT
VERY CLEAN.
IT'S PERFECT WHEN IT ARRIVES
AND IT PUTS ITSELF IN OUR HANDS.
IT HOPES WE'VE LEARNED
SOMETHING FROM YESTERDAY."

John Wayne has taught me many lessons during all my yesterdays spent in his addictive movie company. The importance of individualism, courage and honour. The noble values of truth and self-respect. But my father showed me the way, and my knowledge of the Duke would be nothing without that first inspiration. We are all in darkness without the guiding hands of our teachers.

Reverentially, the Duke's tombstone prints the legend with a background of Alamo and Monument Valley. Clouds hover over the implacable buttes. To the left of the memorial message, the American flag bends at an angle in the breeze. In the foreground, a solitary rider proceeds. But this is no pale horse, and the name sitting on him is no angel of death. For this is John Wayne, the mightiest horseman of the Old West, in fact the mightiest horseman to grace any West,

and the most monumental star the silver screen has seen. I would like to visit the Duke at his peaceful abode, and if I do, a scene from *Back to Bataan* seems appropriate to me, as this would constitute the best method of paying my respects. In the film, a young Filipino is eager to join up with the Duke's Colonel Madden in the final victory push. Wayne explains tactfully to the disappointed boy that his presence is needed away from the hostilities, and that the future of the Philippines as a great nation rests on his staying behind at home. In a gesture that reveals all the Wayne hallmarks of compassion and understanding, the Duke then pins the mark of an officer on the lad, whose joy at his instant promotion is unbridled. They salute one another, as I would undoubtedly say goodbye to Wayne at the tomb with his farewell words from the picture, but this parting of the ways would surely be temporary. Time to take my leave of Big John for now, though. "OK, Colonel. I'll be seeing ya."

John Wayne as Colonel Joseph Madden in Back to Bataan, 1945

Viewing (Twenty John Wayne)

The Big Trail (1930)
Stagecoach (1939)
The Fighting Seabees (1944)
Fort Apache (1948)
Red River (1948)
Sands of Iwo Jima (1949)
She Wore a Yellow Ribbon (1949)
Rio Grande (1950)
The Quiet Man (1952)
Hondo (1953)
The High and the Mighty (1954)
The Searchers (1956)
Legend of the Lost (1957)
Rio Bravo (1959)
The Alamo (1960)
The Longest Day (1962)
McLintock! (1963)
True Grit (1969)
Brannigan (1975)
The Shootist (1976)

Viewing (Ten Lucky Dippers)

Out of the Past (1947) Directed by Jacques
Tourneur Starring **Robert Mitchum**,
Jane Greer and **Kirk Douglas**
Vertigo (1958) Directed by Alfred Hitchcock
Starring **James Stewart**, Kim Novak
and Barbara Bel Geddes
Heller in Pink Tights (1960) Directed by
George Cukor Starring **Sophia Loren**,
Anthony Quinn and Margaret O'Brien
Madigan (1968) Directed by **Don Siegel**
Starring **Richard Widmark, Henry Fonda**
and Anthony Russell
No Way to Treat a Lady (1968) Directed by Jack
Smight Starring **Rod Steiger**, Lee Remick
and George Segal
Breezy (1973) Directed by Clint Eastwood
Starring **William Holden**, Kay Lenz and
Roger C Carmel
Welcome to Arrow Beach (1974) Directed by
Laurence Harvey Starring **Laurence Harvey**,
Joanna Pettet and **Stuart Whitman**
Assault on Precinct 13 (1976) Directed by
John Carpenter Starring Austin Stoker, Darwin
Joston and Laurie Zimmer

Magic (1978) Directed by **Richard Attenborough**
Starring Anthony Hopkins, **Ann-Margret**
and Burgess Meredith
Dressed to Kill (1980) Directed by Brian De Palma
Starring Michael Caine, **Angie Dickinson**
and Nancy Allen.

Suggested further reading and viewing

The Cinema: a History
Keith Reader – 1979 – Hodder and Stoughton
Essential Film: a World History
Daniel Borden, Florian Duijsens, Thomas Gilbert,
and Adele Smith – 2008 – Herbert Press
*Great Movie Moments: Photographs from the
Kobal Collection*
John Russell Taylor – 1987 – Guild Publishing
(London)
The Guinness Book of Film Facts & Feats
Patrick Robertson – 1980 – Guinness Superlatives
Limited
Halliwell's Film Guide: Eighth Edition (Revised)
Ruth Halliwell and John Walker – 1992 – Grafton
Halliwell's Who's Who in the Movies
Leslie Halliwell (Edited by John Walker) – 2001 –
HarperCollins Entertainment
*"Have You Seen…?" – A Personal Introduction to
1,000 Films*
David Thomson – 2008 – Allen Lane
(Penguin Books Ltd)
The History of the Movies
Edited by Ann Lloyd (Consultant Editor David
Robinson) – 1988
Macdonald & Co (Publishers) Ltd
Movies of the 60s
Edited by Jürgen Müller – 2004 – Taschen
The New Biographical Dictionary of Film
David Thomson – 2002 – Little Brown
100 Best Films of the Century
Barry Norman – 1992
Chapmans Publishers Ltd
A Pictorial History of Westerns
Michael Parkinson and Clyde Jeavons – 1972 –
The Hamlyn Publishing
Group Limited
Quinlan's Film Directors
David Quinlan – 1999 – BT Batsford Ltd
RadioTimes Guide to Films 2009

Edited by Sue Robinson – 2008 – BBC
Worldwide Limited
The Rough Guide to Film
Richard Armstrong, Tom Charity, Lloyd Hughes
and Jessica Winter – 2007
Rough Guides (Penguin Books Ltd)
Scene by Scene
Mark Cousins – 2002
Laurence King Publishing Ltd
The Second Virgin Film Guide
James Monaco, James Pallot and BASELINE –
1993 – Virgin Books
Sophia: Living and Loving – Her Own Story
AE Hotchner – 1979 – Michael Joseph Limited
Taxi Driver
Paul Schrader – 1990 – Faber and Faber Limited
The Western
David Carter – 2008 – Kamera Books.

John Wayne poses for the camera during the
filming of The Train Robbers, 1973

£7.99